LIFE BALANCE:

Science and Stories of Everyday Living

KATHLEEN MATUSKA

BALBOA
PRESS

A DIVISION OF HAY HOUSE

Balboa Press books may be ordered through booksellers or by contacting:

Balboa Press
A Division of Hay House
1663 Liberty Drive
Bloomington, IN 47403
www.balboapress.com
1 (877) 407-4847

Because of the dynamic nature of the Internet, any web addresses or links contained in this book may have changed since publication and may no longer be valid. The views expressed in this work are solely those of the author and do not necessarily reflect the views of the publisher, and the publisher hereby disclaims any responsibility for them.

The author of this book does not dispense medical advice or prescribe the use of any technique as a form of treatment for physical, emotional, or medical problems without the advice of a physician, either directly or indirectly. The intent of the author is only to offer information of a general nature to help you in your quest for emotional and spiritual well-being. In the event you use any of the information in this book for yourself, which is your constitutional right, the author and the publisher assume no responsibility for your actions.

Any people depicted in stock imagery provided by Thinkstock are models, and such images are being used for illustrative purposes only.
Certain stock imagery © Thinkstock.

Print information available on the last page.

ISBN: 978-1-504-?92-0 (sc)
ISBN: 978-1-504-?93-7 (hc)
ISBN: 978-1-504-?31-6 (e)

Library of Congress Control Number: 2016907915

Balboa Press rev. date: 05/24/2016

CONTENTS

PREFACE

I spent my entire academic career studying life balance and quality of life with other researchers across the world. I have published my research on life balance and reviewed the literature from various disciplines related to the topic. And I've learned over the years that life balance seems to be a legitimate, scientific construct, different from other constructs like life satisfaction and quality of life. This finding is a big deal because only recently has life balance had any scientific support. Although it was extremely exciting and rewarding for me to be immersed in the science behind life balance, it was frustrating because the only people reading it were other scientists. Doesn't this topic resonate with everyone? This question motivated me to write this book.

This book explores life balance. What is it? Is it possible to live a balanced life? If you live a balanced life, is it a better one? This is not a new topic. You can find people talking about it almost anywhere. What's new in this book is that I will link the science behind life balance to everyday living. This is not a self-help book that provides easy recipe-like directions or optimistic answers for living a balanced life. Rather this book summarizes the scientific research related to life balance and leaves the decision-making and application to you. You will learn why you need to pay attention to stress, different scientific views of a balanced life, common themes about what a balanced life looks like, and the mental and physical health benefits related to living a balanced life. You will have opportunities to assess various aspects of your life and think critically about the way you want to live going forward.

If this appeals to you, read on!

INTRODUCTION

The Most Interesting Things
Happen Over Cocktails

Research related to life balance occurs in many disciplines, like psychology, sociology, family science, and economics, but the perspective I am most affiliated with comes from occupational science. Occupational science explores aspects of occupation (what we do) and how this affects our health and well-being. I have met many of the occupational scientists who are particularly interested in the concept of balance among these occupations. They typically use the term "occupational balance" to refer to the way we configure our occupations or activities and how this configuration ultimately impacts our health and well-being.

I met a group of these scientists at several conferences over the years, and we have become friends and even presented our research together. Each of us looks at the concept of occupational balance or life balance in different ways, and each perspective is equally interesting. I will share their research briefly in chapter 3 when I review various scientific perspectives of a balanced life.

At one of these conferences, Drs. Carita Håkansson, Petra Wagman, and Hans Jonsson from Sweden; Dr. Catherine Backman from Canada; and I met for a happy hour at the conference hotel. Of course, because we have all spent a large part of our careers exploring the same general topic, the conversation was rich and enthusiastic.

At one point, I asked them, "What are the five common characteristics about life (occupational) balance that our research would agree with?"

In less than a minute, we had an agreement. We concurred that the five common characteristics of life (occupational) balance are the following:

1. It is a journey, not a destination. No one ever actually achieves a balanced life that can be sustained over time. We may have periods of relative balance, but we can count on these periods changing regularly.
2. It requires doing things. We cannot solely imagine, think, or feel our way to a balanced life. Whether your life is balanced or not is also determined by what you actually do from day to day.
3. It is good for you. Research indicates a relationship between a balanced life and positive health and well-being outcomes.
4. It is different for everyone. There cannot be a prescription of the right amount of any given activity because activities have different meanings to people and those meanings change depending on the circumstances.
5. Things get in the way. The environment is a big factor in life balance, and we don't always have control over our activity choices.

I feel confident that these five characteristics are on the right track because it was so easy for our group of scientists, who have spent years examining the topic, to agree with them. The chapters in part 1 will set the stage by discussing background information about why you should listen to me, what the current state of the research is, and why we should care about life balance. The chapters in part 2 will discuss each of the five characteristics of life balance that were agreed upon at our cocktail hour. Sprinkled throughout the book will be short stories in the form of case studies that I created to illustrate a main point. I also interviewed people from various slices of life, and their real stories are highlighted at the end of some chapters. Their names were changed, and other identifying information has been removed to protect their privacy.

Contact information and affiliation of the four researchers contributing to the five characteristics of life balance include:

Catherine Backman, PhD, FCAOT
Professor, Department of Occupational
Science & Occupational Therapy
The University of British Columbia,
T325-2211 Wesbrook Mall, Vancouver, BC V6T 2B5,
Canada
and
Research Scientist, Arthritis Research Canada
Richmond, BC,
Canada

Petra Wagman, PhD, Reg. OT
Assistant Professor and Program Coordinator
of Occupational Therapy, Department of
Rehabilitation, School of Health and Welfare
Jönköping University
Box 1026, 551 11 Jönköping
Sweden

Hans Jonsson, PhD, Reg. OT
Associate Professor, Division of Occupational Therapy
Karolinska Institutet
Fack 23200
SE-141 83 Huddinge
Sweden

Carita Håkansson, PhD, Reg. OT
Associate Professor, Department of Occupational
and Environmental Medicine
Lund University
Box 117, SE-221 00 Lund, Sweden

PART 1

SETTING THE STAGE

CHAPTER 1

Why Should You Listen to Me?

I have a couple of reasons why you should listen to me about life balance:

1. I made a long career about the study of the topic.
2. My life story led me to the topic in the first place.

My educational background and life experiences have influenced my unique view of the world. Both inspired me to write this book. Each experience, whether deliberate or accidental, took me down a path that intersected with another route and moved me in ways I could not have imagined.

In 1979, my new husband Tom and I moved to a one-room cabin in the woods in northern Minnesota. We naïvely jumped into the lifestyle mostly because we thought it would be cheap living, but also because we loved nature and simple living. The cabin was the size of a single-car garage, without plumbing or electricity. Our compact stove and refrigerator were fueled with propane, and for heat, we used a small woodstove. In order to survive the cold and snowy Minnesota winters, we needed a large supply of wood to burn, so we spent many hours in the woods, often on snowshoes, cutting and splitting wood and dragging it back to the cabin. We used lanterns for light and gathered water from a nearby creek.

Of course, in the winter, the creek was frozen over, so we had to break a hole in the ice to scoop out the water we needed. The biggest challenge for me was using an outhouse for our other plumbing needs. Toilet seats become frosted in the winter, so to ease the discomfort, we put strips of carpet on the seat to prevent it from sticking to our skin. I didn't like going to the outhouse when it was dark, and even though I knew black bears hibernated in the winter, I imagined meeting one between the cabin and outhouse. I always took a flashlight with me.

Our lifestyle was very simple. I had a professional job as an occupational therapist in town. I would wake up early, put wood in the stove because it had burned down between and was getting cold, and drive nine miles to work, where I took a shower and groomed before starting the day.

Tom had a few temporary jobs. When he was not working for others, he would fur-trap, log, and ice-fish. In the other seasons, we grew and harvested our own vegetables, hunted for meat, and lived off the land as much as we could. It was surprising to me that, without TV or other distractions, we were never bored. In any season, our days were always full with simple tasks for survival, and once the chores were done, we would take long hikes or cross-country ski in the woods.

We lived in the cabin for two and a half years. When our first daughter was born, it became clear to us that we wouldn't find the kind of work and careers we were hoping for. There are many stories to tell about this experience. (Maybe that will be my next book.) But suffice to say, I didn't know at the time how it would shape my life and career path. Looking back, the main takeaway was that we both realized how little was needed for happiness. We didn't have many material goods simply because there was no place to put them. Going forward into my life, I always had the confidence that a simple life is just fine, and it shaded the way I looked at overstimulated, overstressed lifestyles.

I am an occupational therapist. This educational background is significant to my final story because of the lens through which occupational therapists view the world. We view people and their quality of life by whether or not they are able to engage in everyday occupations or other activities that bring meaning and satisfaction to their lives. Being able to do what we want to do in life is as powerful as taking medication, eating nutritiously, or exercising. The ability to do is fundamental to dignity, self-worth, and life fulfillment. Of course, when people have barriers that prevent this important doing, such as mental or physical disabilities, then occupational therapists help them find ways to remove those barriers or create other ways to do what they want to do. You will see in this book how doing is one of the foundations for living a balanced life.

After we moved from the cabin to the Twin Cities, I took advantage of the opportunity to go back to school for a graduate degree in public health on a part-time basis while growing our family. Public health stretched my focus from individual health to community or societal health. I began to examine lifestyles and stress and discovered how political, economic, and social structures influenced our choices and affected our health and well-being. At the time I was a mother of three. I was working part time, taking graduate courses, and remaining active in the neighborhood. I was also grieving my mother's unexpected and early death.

I was interested in women's roles and finding out how women were coping with all the demands on their time. How do they find the balance between just the right amount of activities to remain stimulated and interested in their lives and way too much activity, a lifestyle that puts them at risk for illness? Right in the middle of this period, I must have been stressed enough to significantly lower my immune response because, at a healthy age of thirty-three, I got shingles. Apparently a by-product of chicken pox, the virus sits dormant until your immune response is unable to suppress it. Stress suppresses the immune response, and we get sick.

When mixing a public health perspective with an occupational therapy lens, I began to wonder about preventing illness and disability through healthy lifestyles. Lifestyles are the configuration of daily activities that we create for ourselves; the mix of activities chosen may be healthy or not. I had the opportunity to experience two very different lifestyles, both with their own challenges and rewards. The configuration of daily activities I had when living in the cabin consisted of chores for survival. We worked to meet our daily needs. The rewards were immediate, having warm water or adequate heat. The challenges were plenty, such as surviving in the cold and darkness, and it certainly felt stressful at times. The configuration of activities when living in town, raising small children, working, and going to school, consisted of caring for others and trying to squeeze in time for myself without anyone noticing. The rewards were very meaningful but not always immediate. The challenges were constant, and stress was often high.

I thought deeply about how I was living my life and what I was doing from day to day. I wondered if one lifestyle was healthier than another. Is it important to have a balance between activities that meet your own needs and others'? If such a balance of activities would be best, what does that look like?

Fast-forward a few years. I am on the faculty of an occupational therapy program at St. Catherine University in St. Paul, Minnesota. Research with my colleagues, Dr. Virgil Mathoiwetz and Dr. Marcia Finlayson, gave me firsthand exposure to people who were struggling to create satisfactory lifestyles. We ran educational groups for people who had multiple sclerosis and felt that fatigue was one of their most disabling symptoms. They had stories about spending all their energy on things that had to get done, like going to work and doing chores, but at a cost of giving up all other pleasurable activities that gave them joy. When they pushed too hard one day for a special event, they needed two days of complete rest to recover. They started losing friends, and their family members were getting frustrated with them.

In our courses, they learned how to make the most of their limited energy by using it on activities that were most important to them.[1] We also showed them how to build energy by resting at strategic points in their day. We found that, once the participants learned and used the energy-saving strategies, they reported less fatigue and reported a higher quality of life.[2]

One of the women in the group said she had to quit her job because of severe fatigue that made her immobile after a six-hour workday. She wanted to feel like she was contributing to the family, so she tried to keep up the house and mow the lawn, a job that used to belong to her husband. She came to the group feeling defeated and distraught because, after doing one or two projects or mowing the lawn, that would be it for the day. Our group taught her to plan her activities to make the most of her limited energy.[3] She decided to mow the lawn in the morning before the heat of the day, as heat also increases fatigue for people who have MS, and to break the one-hour job into two thirty-minute sessions. She cut the front yard one day and the backyard another day. Then after mowing, she would rest before she felt tired and hydrate. We also showed her how to plan for other activities that could be broken down into smaller tasks.

In the end, using a variety of these strategies, she was able to accomplish much more and felt like she was contributing to her family. The success of these interventions reinforced to me that examining our activity patterns and prioritizing activities that are most meaningful to us is extremely important to our well-being. Creating a healthy lifestyle starts with understanding what we do every day and deliberately modifying it to meet our needs.

Then I started reading anything I could that related to life balance and tinkered around with some beginning ideas. I presented some early thoughts at a conference and met Dr. Charles Christiansen, who was also interested in the topic. We collaborated with a comprehensive review of the literature related to life balance.[4]

There was very little on the topic of life balance itself, so we had to piece together information from psychology, sociology, family studies, and occupational science literature on the topic of what constitutes a good life. What we found led us to a first version of a proposed lifestyle balance theory and moved me to take it further by creating a model and measure that I tested in my PhD studies.[5]

The accumulated knowledge I've gained from my education and life experiences, along with the contribution from other scientists' views, are the foundation of this book.

CHAPTER 2

Why Should You Care?

Stress wasn't something that Jennifer worried about. When she married Stan, her life was exactly as she always planned. Her work as a tax lawyer and Stan's career as a graphic designer kept them stimulated and financially secure. Things started to get a little more complicated as their family grew. With three children—ages one, four, and six years old—and both of them working full time, Jennifer began to experience pressure from multiple sources. She worked it out with her boss to start early and leave every day at four o'clock so she could pick up the kids from school and daycare and then take them to their events.

Although that arrangement helped on the family end, she felt like doors closed on the work end. Sarah knew she lost favor with her boss because all the best clients were referred to others who could put in the hours, and she felt awkward and misunderstood by her colleagues when she would leave early as they stayed working.

Stan is also pressured because he has a 10:00 a.m. to 6:00 p.m. work shift that is nonnegotiable at this time. Jennifer comes home exhausted but has to cook dinner every night because of Stan's schedule. Their children have become very fussy eaters, and making a nutritious meal for them generally turns into a frustrating situation, including shouts and tears. Jennifer has gained ten pounds in the last four months and hasn't felt like exercising. Their oldest son is having trouble in first grade, such as hitting others and being disruptive in class. And their four-year-old was recently diagnosed with asthma. It feels like everything is falling apart, and Jennifer is so stressed and tired that she wonders if work, marriage, and family are worth it.

You might be able to relate to Jennifer's story, at least the part about the stress buildup. There are times in life when stress seems to pile on and doesn't let up. Jennifer's life ebbs and flows with stress, but somehow she manages to get through and finds moments when things feel balanced, at least until the next stressful series of events happen. It is not easy to find balance in life, especially in Western cultures where fast-paced living and consumerism set up a perfect context for stressful, lonely, unbalanced lives.

I wanted to understand how to reduce overall stress, but I resisted the idea of examining lifestyles for compliance with a prescribed regimen of activities in order to be healthy. A lifestyle diet with specific hours of sleep, leisure, work, exercise, and relaxation just didn't seem realistic or sustainable. What I found was that most research on life balance agreed that there is no prescription of daily activities that would be considered balanced, like the well-known food pyramid. Generally research points to the importance of considering the outcome of life for each unique individual—such as contentment, happiness, and accomplishment—rather than the specific repertoire of activities that people engage in on a daily basis.

Most scientists agree that one of the most important outcomes of a balanced life is lower stress. That makes sense because, if the way you are living results in good health, happy relationships, and overall contentment, you would probably have lower stress than people dealing with chronic health issues and dysfunctional relationships. You can find excellent books about stress almost anywhere. You can also find reams of research on the physiological consequences of chronic stress on your body.

Stress Can Be Good

It is impossible to eliminate all stress from your life. In fact, according to researchers in positive psychology, it wouldn't be a good idea anyway. Hans Selye, a renowned endocrinologist in the mid-twentieth century examined the physiological stress response and determined there is negative stress (distress) and positive stress (eustress).[6]

Imagine how dull life would be if you never experienced the excitement and happiness associated with positive things, like your marriage, first day of work, travel, or birth of your child(ren). These are actually very stressful situations, but stress in the right circumstances can be considered the spice of life. It can be what creates challenge, suspense, and excitement.

Stress can be a motivator, and that force might explain why we developed a stress response to begin with. Stress helps our brain to focus so we can react to potential dangerous situations in the wild, and this might mean, for instance, trying to escape from a predator. A release of adrenaline speeds up your heart rate and metabolism. In the short run, this results in increased reactions and reflexes, while also acting as a painkiller, meaning you can have better endurance. This level of stress would be a boost for an athlete or help you get through an exhausting public presentation.

I have embraced the idea that the butterflies I feel in my chest before an important speech or meeting will help me do a better job because I'm charged up. Of course, eventually the speech is over, and the stress response subsides. Good stress should be short-lived and not something that exists over a prolonged period. Otherwise it becomes bad stress.

Stress Can Be Bad

Prolonged stress is bad stress and damages almost every cell in your body. The body tries to achieve stability through change, and the physiological response is called "allostasis."[7] Generally the physiological responses are activated to survive the stressor and help us cope. However, if the stress persists over a long period, the accumulated physiological responses builds up. For example, blood pressure responds to the body's need for blood flow given various levels of physical activity. Once you perceive a threat in the environment, your blood pressure also increases to prepare you to manage the threat. This is very useful when you need the blood flow during a race, but it's less useful when your threat is an upcoming exam and you respond by sitting and eating.

Prolonged high blood pressure, when not used for physical activity, will lead to serious health conditions. Similarly the other metabolic, hormonal, neurologic, and immunological responses to stress have protective effects in the short run but accumulate over time if not spent. These accumulated responses make up allostatic load,[7] the wear and tear on the body over time.

Stress Buffers

Since it is impossible to totally eliminate stress, the next best thing is to try to create a lifestyle that at least buffers some of the negative effects. That's not an easy task when you look at the pace of modern life. Lots of things like high credit card debt, urban sprawl, long commutes, and high divorce and obesity rates reflect the lifestyles of Americans that are stressful. Some of the stress we experience is under our control to change; some of it isn't. For example, you can make a deliberate attempt to leave the house earlier to avoid the stress of being late for work. But there isn't much you can do to change the stress of living with a disability or nurturing a family member with a mental illness.

When you are stressed, you can either add to the problem or reduce your stress. Sometimes people think they are coping with stress by engaging in negative behaviors, like smoking, overeating, using drugs or alcohol, or acting hostile or moody. You know which vice belongs to you. And you also know these don't really help. The challenge is to replace those negative actions with activities that will actually help you.

You can do a lot of things to reduce the harmful effects of stress on your body, even if you can't always eliminate the source of the stressor. Generally they are called "stress buffers." In other words, if your life feels out of control with stress and you cannot see how it will get better in the near future, you can do a few things that will reduce the effects on your health. Research supports several attitudes or feelings that buffer stress, like feeling competent or having a sense of purpose,[8] but that isn't always helpful if you can't muster up those attitudes when you need them.

I prefer the practical approaches that help you know what to do in moments of stress. For example, exercise is a powerful stress buffer.[9] Have you ever felt really stressed or upset and then went for a walk or run and noticed how much better you felt afterward? It is hard to feel like exercising when life feels out of control, but at least it is something you can do rather than trying to think or feel your way out of a stressful situation. Exercise also helps us sleep better, and sleep in itself can be a buffer.[10] There is increasing research about the restorative effects of sleep, especially when it comes to buffering the stress response.[11]

Another powerful stress buffer is doing things with family or friends, especially leisure activities.[12] We need people in our lives.[13] If you find you are often alone in your stress, you might want to reach out to someone, not necessarily to discuss your situation, but just to have a distraction and divert your attention to something positive. Exercise and social activities are things you can actually do, even if you don't really feel like it at the moment.

Robert

Life balance is "living life in the present, not dwelling on the past or worrying about the future." Robert had some peaks and valleys in his life balance journey. A sixty-five-year-old professor at a major research university, he is just beginning his phased retirement schedule. He was very motivated and energized by his work to a point where he felt it might have contributed to his divorce after twenty-one years of marriage.

Early in his marriage, Robert went to graduate school and completed a PhD while working as an assistant professor. This was a significant challenge for life balance, especially when he also had two small children. He worked with a focused passion to finish his dissertation, followed by the same drive to meet many research expectations of a tenure track faculty member. His natural personality is to be very goal-driven, organized, and persistent, which served him well to accomplish the many milestones in his progressive career. He also has a natural tendency to prefer even emotion and low-keeled approaches, and he has avoided lots of high emotion and conflict. This combination proved difficult for his wife, who was high on the emotional expression side. She needed a different kind of communication and was equally as driven in her career. Looking back, Robert sees that both prioritized time with their children over time together.

Robert admits that those early married years with small children and a demanding career was very imbalanced at times and he could feel the effects of stress. He is also quick to emphasize, however, that there were many wonderful and peaceful moments with his family and he is proud of the many things they have done together. In his view, they were a happy, healthy family who had lots going on and stressful schedules. But he thought that was no different than anyone else.

Then in one year, Robert hit a low point when his marriage ended in divorce, his father died, the program at the university was in crisis, and he was forced to take the lead of the program during the crisis. Robert said he couldn't sleep at night because his mind was racing with questions, he was too stressed to do regular exercise, he was too exhausted and hurt to go out with friends, and everything that brought him joy was put on hold.

After a couple years of personal struggle, Robert reflected on what he had learned and decided to be proactive about making changes in his life. He set some small and big goals around finding a new romantic partner, starting with learning new ways to be a better communicator and open to others. He also wanted some practical solutions for managing the stress he felt, so he exercised more regularly and took courses in stress reduction with inconsistent success in practicing the strategies.

He tried dating, but nothing clicked until he met Sharon, whom a friend had introduced him to. Sharon had a low-key disposition that suited Robert beautifully, and both loved to travel. This was a high point in Robert's life balance, and he had a noticeable reduction in stress. He found the love of his life and felt he was growing personally and professionally.

Ten months after they were married, Sharon was diagnosed with breast cancer. Four years later she died. When I asked Robert about life balance at this time in his life, I was surprised by his answer. He said he was "called" for being Sharon's caretaker and viewed his service to her as a blessing and an opportunity for him to be the best man he could be. Robert looks back on that time as sad but deeply meaningful. And this experience with Sharon shaped his identity and what he is doing with the rest of his life.

Robert is a planner, and thinks logically. After Sharon died, he knew he had to rethink his future because he didn't plan on being

alone. In a very logical way, Robert decided on a phased retirement with a little less work each year so he could have time to slowly adjust to time off. He had three major goals: to find and nurture meaningful relationships, to find meaningful activity to replace work, and to improve his overall health.

Improving his health was easiest to do because he had more time to exercise and pay attention to healthy eating. And with less stress from work, he is finally able to sleep well. The other two goals are a work in progress. He has lots of interests and has volunteered for his church and community. He loves sporting events, art, and theatre. Finding enjoyable leisure activities is not difficult for Robert, but he would also like meaningful service activities to replace some of his former work time.

Going forward, Robert is continuing to take classes that will help him live more in the present and be a better communicator in current and future relationships. He thinks his next step is to try online dating, but he is slow to sign up. In the meantime, he will continue staying as active as possible, so once he is fully retired, he will find daily fulfillment.

Boost My Buffers!

1. List one or two of the biggest stressors you anticipate this week:

2. Which of the following negative behaviors have you used in the past to deal with your stress?
   - Use of drugs or alcohol
   - Smoking
   - Overeating
   - Withdrawal or refusal to interact
   - Shouting/arguing/being generally nasty to live with
   - Overworking
   - My own unique bad behaviors

3. Choose one thing in each activity category below that you will commit to doing this week to boost your buffers. Then start doing a buffer activity every week to replace the negative behaviors above.
   a. Sleep: What I will do to improve my sleep?
      - Go to bed a half hour earlier
      - Keep the bed for sleeping (not working on the computer and so forth)
      - Take a hot, relaxing bath before bed
      - Do some deep breathing exercises
      - Make a mental list of everything you are grateful for
      - Other

   b. Exercise: What I will do to move my body?
      - Walk/run/hike at least thirty minutes
      - Take a fitness class (aerobics, yoga, and so forth)
      - Lift weights
      - Ride a bike
      - Participate in water sports (swim, canoe, kayak, and so forth)
      - Engage in team sports
      - Other favorite physical activity

c. Social activities: What I will do to stay connected?
- Call family or friends who live far away
- Go out to a restaurant with someone
- Invite people over for an activity
- Talk to your neighbors when they are outside
- Go to a movie, play, or musical event with someone
- Other favorite social event

CHAPTER 3

What Is Life Balance?

The term "life balance" describes almost anything related to a good life. In scientific literature, almost every scientist describes the construct of life balance differently. So what is the point of discussing it then? Like any other positive attribute—health, happiness, well-being, or life satisfaction, to name a few—people seek anything that resembles or contributes to what they think it is, even if they can't define it well. These positive attributes are experienced differently by everyone, and none have universally agreed-upon definitions. But people still seek them out.

Popular Ideas about Life Balance

Have you ever picked up a magazine or book that displayed an enticing topic like losing weight without dieting, understanding the opposite sex, or creating a stress-free life? And you really wanted to make all of those things happen so you could hardly wait to read about the secrets. I have done this more times than I am comfortable admitting, but I wanted to believe in tricks and secrets for achieving these life attributes. Not once have I been impressed with the contents of the articles. Usually I am left feeling like the answers provided are too broad and feel too much like common sense. Answers like "build more downtime into your routine" or "open and honest communication is the key to understanding your significant other" leave me flat. This is not enlightening information; nor do I find it helpful. We may know the right way to do things. We just don't do them because life gets in the way, and people and events have an uncanny way of interfering with our plans for self-improvement.

I believe that no one gets it right every time. In other words, whether it is our health, our relationships, our work, or any other aspect of life, sometimes things go well (and we could write one of those articles), but many times life events do not go as planned. All caregivers of animals, children, aging parents, or others would be first to admit that they are rarely in control enough to follow all the good advice they know about. Things happen. People get sick, personalities bump up against each other, things break, and we all get tired. My brother said he watched our parents raise eight kids, and he had ideas of how he could improve on that with his own children. He laughs when he admits that the one missing piece he didn't know was that he'd have to do these improved parenting ideas when he was too tired to care.

If living a balanced life or any other goal were easy, there wouldn't be 157 million hits when the term "life balance" is used in a Google search (October 2014). Clearly there is an interest in the topic, and people keep hunting. When scanning some of the Internet sites about life balance, people are obviously talking about different things. For example, we can purchase apps for iPhones that remind us about our goals and priorities and help with time management to balance responsibilities of work, home, and play. Other sites focus on health-related topics, such as website programs that encourage members to participate in healthy activities or sell nutritional products and vitamins as a way to achieve life balance. Many sites provide tips on managing attitudes and thought processes to feel more balanced, while others focus on time use and seeking more time for self. You can find people identifying themselves as life coaches who will work with you to help you achieve your goals.

The most common way to conceptualize life balance is whether you are satisfied in the many domains of your life: home, family, work, recreation, or finances. The domains of life are different among authors, but the idea that satisfaction should be similar across all domains is gaining acceptance. Generally these authors provide a way for you to examine your life balance by completing a wheel of life or something similar. You fill out your level of satisfaction in each domain represented as spokes on the wheel, and you end up with a picture of your life balance. A ranking of ten (outside edge) means it is ideal with decreasing levels of satisfaction as you move toward the center.

When there are uneven levels of satisfaction, you end up with a bumpy wheel that illustrates areas in your life needing attention. For Jennifer, whom you met in the previous chapter, she was relatively satisfied in the following areas:

- Money: Both had good jobs.
- Physical environment: She loved her home.
- Career: She likes being a lawyer.

The bumpiness of her wheel comes in with low levels of satisfaction in fun, recreation, friends, and family, as she was too busy.

She was least satisfied with the following:

- Her health: She was gaining weight and stopping her exercises.
- Her relationship with her husband and personal growth: She was giving up her hobbies.

This exercise puts a visual emphasis on what she already knows but is intended to help focus her plans for improvement. After examining popular writings about life balance in magazines and websites, I felt there was little depth and looked for more scientific evidence and substance on the topic.

The Science of Life Balance

You would think that scientists would be able to rally around the idea of life balance and give us some clear ideas about what it is and whether it is worth having, if possible. But the science is still too new, and there are many definitions and theories about life balance and no clear agreement. However, the majority of scientists support the idea that some form of life balance is indeed desirable. Most of the background theory comes from positive psychology, a branch of science that studies the positive attributes of people and how these contribute to well-being, hardiness, or resilience. Positive psychology attempts to answer questions like, "What values, characteristics, strengths, virtues, or talents do people bring to their lives that help them overcome hardships and flourish?"

The same question can be applied to managing stress. What kinds of lifestyles and attitudes will allow someone to remain relatively happy and healthy, given generally stressful modern lives? Here is where the link is made to living a balanced life. Although you will see that there is a lot to be learned about life balance, most of the science points to the idea that it is related to better health and reduced effects of stress.

Fulfilling Your Roles

A role is the set of expectations about how you are supposed to act when you are with others. When you are being a mother or father, certain ways of behaving set you apart from when you are in the role of friend or lover. Everyone holds a variety of roles: friend, daughter, son, lover, spouse, mother, or employee, to name a few. Some scientists believe that a good way to know if you are living a balanced life is whether or not you feel satisfied with how well you are fulfilling your roles. In fact research has consistently found that participation in valued roles is related to life satisfaction and well-being.[14]

Scientists have also found that, when roles are in conflict, there is increased stress.[15] This is easy to imagine when you think about the occasions when there are too many demands on your time, for example, your work deadline is looming, you have to prepare a large family event, and your child is sick. Yes, there will be increased stress. Maybe it would be best to have fewer roles so there is less conflict between them. Interestingly the opposite appears to be the case.

Having more social roles seems to give people the necessary level of reinforcement to get through stressful times easier. When roles are in conflict, such as parent and employee, people who have other valued roles can at least find some satisfaction and support to get them through the conflict. Social support is increased when you have more roles. If you have a strong connection with your neighbors, your church, and your local community organizations, you will have more options for support than those who do not have those roles.[14] When people felt they had a good balance among multiple roles, they seemed to have less stress, lower rates of depression, and higher self-esteem than people who felt their roles were in conflict with one another.

How do people make that balance among roles happen? The answer to that question is not known yet, but we can speculate that people who have balanced roles may be particularly good at fulfilling several roles at one time. Things like preparing dinner while including your children in the preparation fulfills homemaker and mother roles. Answering email from your phone while waiting for a doctor appointment or walking the dog together with your spouse fulfills more than one role at a time. These role-balanced people had a perception that they fulfilled all their roles with ease and satisfaction and were fully engaged in performing all their roles.[16]

It is challenging to think about life balance only through the lens of fulfilling roles because activities chosen to fulfill roles will vary among individuals. For example, one mother may feel that cooking nutritious meals for regular family dinners is important, whereas another may find that less important and emphasize taking her children to activities that often interfere with regular meals. Thus, for one mother but not another, cooking is important, and if the pressures of life make it so that she cannot cook as much as she would like to, she may report feeling imbalanced.

How the Activity Is Experienced

An entirely different way of thinking about life balance is to pay attention to the activities we do and how they are experienced. Scientists in Sweden[17] proposed that life balance is best understood as a balanced mix of types of everyday experiences. They suggested that how an activity is experienced is more important than the activity itself. In other words, no matter what you are doing, it probably falls into one of three possible experiences:

1. This is when the activity you are doing is highly challenging but matched to your high skills. It is intense but rewarding. This might be something like giving a speech, playing a very challenging game, writing a paper for a class, or creating a work of art or music. You can imagine that, for this kind of activity, you like the challenge because you have just enough ability to succeed in it. This type of experience usually results in the state termed as "flow."[18] This positive state is one where you lose track of time, you are deeply engaged in the activity, and you are not focused on anything but what you are doing.[19]

2. This is when the activity you are doing is highly challenging but not matched to your skill level. This activity experience is somewhat stressful and stretches your ability level. This could be different for everyone, but for me, it would be activities related to fixing things, where I can probably do it eventually but I'm terribly incompetent, or negotiating new technology. It is not that these experiences are to be avoided; in fact, they push us to grow and learn. But in the short-term experience, they are stressful. Eventually activities in this category can become part of the first category, where your skill has caught up to the challenge. Almost all new learning starts with this type of experience.

3. This is when the activity you are doing is not very challenging for you. These are the routine things you do where little effort is required. Accomplishing morning dressing and grooming routines,

walking the dog, watching TV, and doing household tasks might fit in this category. These could either be viewed as highly relaxing and restorative activities or highly boring and unfulfilling.

Drs. Persson and Jonsson theorize that all three experience types are important for achieving balance in life, meaning that none is intrinsically positive or negative. The three experience types have different relationships to each other and are needed within the total context of everyday experience. Once you have finished a very challenging task, it can feel good to do something mundane and restful. Yet, if you don't have anything to relax from, the restful experience can feel boring and lead to life dissatisfaction.

If any of the three experiences is too dominating, an imbalance arises that, in the long term, might risk developing into a destructive process, one that would lead to burnout on one end or lethargy and depression on the other. Too much challenge will result in the stress of anxiety; too little challenge results in the stress of boredom.[17]

The "Just Right" Variation in Activities

You will know when you have the right variation in your activities to feel balanced. We all need change and variability to keep us interested and engaged in life. Sometimes it feels just right to stay at home and watch a good movie with a bowl of popcorn, but if you did that every night, it would feel dull and depressing. Variety is the spice of life. You will also know if you are spending too much time doing one thing and not enough time doing others. Sometimes housework can feel very rewarding, especially if it has been a while since it was done. But if it becomes too much of a time burden and interferes with other fun activities, the feeling of imbalance surfaces.

Swedish researchers found these ideas to be legitimate in people's perceptions of balance.[20] They found in multiple studies that balance is subjective and multidimensional and related to health.[21] People experience balance when they feel they are having the right amount of activities and the appropriate variation among them.[22] The right variation needs to occur across different areas, such as rest, play, and work, and with different characteristics, such as highly valued activities, obligatory tasks that must be done, and discretionary activities that are for pleasure. Finally people want to feel like they have enough time to do these activities.[23] In other words, squeezing in ten minutes to play the piano (discretionary activity) may not help you feel balanced if you really wanted to play longer.

Needing variability or having a mix of activities seems to be a common theme with research on life balance. If you are or were a parent of young children, it may be difficult to imagine feeling balanced because the needs of your family often override your needs. Canadian researchers interviewed working parents of young children who expressed two distinct dimensions of life balance.[24] One dimension was expressed as "managing life," the satisfaction felt when engaging in activities for the benefit of the family.

However, those activities limited their engagement in personal activities that they also valued. Parents viewed having a mix of activities as another dimension important for life balance. You can see that these are opposing forces, but parents seem to value all the things they do to keep the family going as long as there are moments of "me time" sprinkled in.

Parenting adds its own unique challenge to living. Now imagine what it might be like to have the same challenges with the additional burden of managing a chronic illness or disability. People who had rheumatoid arthritis (RA) in Vienna, Austria, shared their stories about how they tried to achieve life balance.[25]

Similar to the dimensions expressed by working parents, the participants with RA felt a mix of activity characteristics was important for their health and well-being. They also saw a need for a mix of activities related to caring for self versus others and individual versus community activities. This group also highlighted the need to have a balance between challenging and relaxing activities.

The research mentioned so far conceptualizes life balance as one end of a spectrum and life imbalance on the other. In other words, your life is somewhere on the spectrum, either closer to balance or nearer to imbalance. A group of Canadian researchers questioned whether life balance and imbalance should be on a single spectrum and proposed they are two distinct dimensions that can coexist. (One scale indicated the level of life balance; a second scale indicated the level of life imbalance).[26] For example, you might feel that your daily pattern fits with your interests and values (a balanced state) but does not fit with the environmental expectations (unbalanced).

These researchers found that conflict among activities is related to lower life satisfaction, but balance or harmony among activities is not related to life satisfaction. It seems that we notice when we are not able to engage in activities the way we want, and it is reflected in dissatisfaction, but once we have harmony among activities, it is taken for granted.[26]

Living with Integrity

Another way to view a balanced life is one where your actions and everyday activities are in harmony with your personal values, or living with integrity. This view originated with Canadian researchers who believed the metaphor of balance is too dualistic. You are either in or out of balance.[27] This idea obscures the fundamental characteristics and nature of balance, supposedly representing an ideal state. They proposed that living with integrity involves choosing everyday activities that matter the most, and the extent to which we can design lives consistent with our values will influence the degree to which we feel a sense of balance and well-being.

This isn't easy. It means reconciling and prioritizing what we choose to do on the basis of personal values. How many of us actually take the time and attention to think about our activity choices from day to day and check them with our values? The first step is to be clear about what our values are. If one of your top values is spending time with family, choosing activities that conflict with that value, such as working longer hours, will create a feeling of imbalance and stress. The second step—and probably the most difficult—is to consciously prioritize your top values and become assertive enough to say no to things that conflict with them. This means living with the consequences of making choices that may let others down or incur disapproval from others. However, the failure to make activity choices from a stance of personal values over time will negatively affect our well-being and health.[27]

Life Balance and Happiness

If people were given opportunities to create lives that were satisfactory to them, would they have better overall life outcomes than people who cannot create satisfactory lives? Most of the science described above addresses the activities themselves, that is, if they fulfil roles, how they are experienced, or if they matched your values.

Another possible way to think about life balance is to forget about the activities you engage in and focus entirely on the outcomes of your life or how you feel about your life. If you can say, "Yes, I have a pretty good life," even when you are in a stressful period, that means you are balanced. One sociologist from the Netherlands explored these ideas and asserts that balance would be best viewed as satisfaction with life as a whole, that is, in happiness.[28] Satisfaction in particular domains of life does not mean balanced living, such as having high job satisfaction if it is costing low satisfaction with family life. This perspective seems to accept the idea that there is too much variation from day to day and year to year and people are capable of having an overall sense of happiness even if their daily lives aren't exactly as they would like.

Life Balance and Need Satisfaction

Another life outcome other than happiness that might be a good measure of life balance is whether your needs are met or not. One could argue that happiness would be difficult to attain if you are hungry, if no one cares for you, or if you have nothing to look forward to. But which needs are most essential?

Psychologists are still debating which human needs are most essential for quality of life and well-being. In spite of this, there seems to be some broad commonalities across needs theories that may be helpful for us to think about. Most theories suggest, to have a satisfying life, we need positive relationships, some kind of autonomy or positive identity, and a sense of competence. People who experienced balanced need satisfaction (similar scores across need areas) reported higher well-being than those with greater variability in need satisfaction.[29]

In other words, the best outcome for people is when all three needs are equally satisfied. When people were satisfied with how much time they spent in daily activities, they had significantly higher need satisfaction and personal well-being than those who had imbalanced time use.[30] Life balance could be viewed as satisfaction with the amount of time spent in activities that meet our needs.

My Definition of Life Balance

Think about the various perspectives of life balance discussed in this chapter.

1. Write down some words that came out of the various perspectives that you can relate to the most, for example, time use, needs, experience, roles, life satisfaction, and outcomes.
2. Now write down some things that you consider essential to a balanced life
3. Review what you have written in both sections and complete the following sentences:
   a. In my opinion, a balanced life is one where …
   b. I'm living a balanced life when I am doing …
   c. If I live a balanced life, the following outcomes will occur:

CHAPTER 4

The Life Balance Model

My early thinking about life balance came out of shared work with a colleague, Dr. Charles Christiansen. Based on a comprehensive review of the literature[4] and our backgrounds in occupational science, we proposed a model that is based on the idea that a balanced life is one where our everyday patterns of activity meet our basic needs.[5] Instead of being prescriptive about the amount of time we should spend in work, leisure, sleep, and exercise, we felt that the life outcome of our activities was most important. At the end of the day, if what you do meets your needs, you have a balanced life. This proposed model is what I took with me in my PhD program at the University of Minnesota to refine the constructs and test the assumptions. In the end, I developed the life balance model (LBM),[31] which I will describe in this chapter.

You Have to Do It

It starts with the idea that a lifestyle is made up of all the things we do from day to day. This doing is what is important and the most honest way to examine lifestyles. In other words, we may want to exercise and think we will, but we're not exercising until our feet hit the pavement. We cannot think or feel our way into a healthy lifestyle. We have to actually do it. People don't always remember honestly how they've spent their time. For example, it's common to hear people say, "I have absolutely no time to exercise," yet they are forgetting they spend two hours in the evening watching TV. The first idea in the LBM is that life balance is best understood by the actual pattern of activities people engage in, not how they think or feel they are doing.

We Only Have Twenty-four Hours

The next idea is that we all make choices about how to use the twenty-four hours available to us each day. We have to parcel the time up into a reasonable schedule so we can accomplish the things we need and want to do. There's the rub. Sometimes it feels like we spend all of our time doing work, housework, or caregiving and don't have any time left for the more leisure or enjoyable activities.

A balanced life would be one where there is a match between how much time you want to engage in activities and how much time you actually engage in those activities. As you can imagine, it would be impossible to prescribe what that should look like for each person.

I love to spend time in my vegetable garden, weeding and pruning. That would be tortuous work for someone else who would rather be playing an instrument, for example. It is not the activity itself that matters; it is the match between your actual and desired time doing it.

It is not easy to take control over the limited twenty-four hours, making sure the time is spent in ways that are satisfying to you. I'm suggesting that this is a skill and involves the ability to know yourself and what is important to you, to set and achieve goals, and to have tenacity about what you need and want to do. I believe the skills required to create a balanced life can be learned.

Our Four Basic Needs

Of course you may have spotted the one flaw in the idea of a balanced life being a match between desired and actual time spent in activities. Imagine this scenario: Sandra, a married woman with two children, works twelve-hour days, six days a week, and feels very content because her husband does most of the childcare, and she feels fulfilled in her job. She wants to spend that much time working. On her one day off, she sleeps in and then plays video games to relax. She is doing exactly what she wants. (There is a match.) But unfortunately she is gaining weight and not physically healthy. And her husband and children are very unhappy, and eventually her relationships will deteriorate. Sometimes people choose activity patterns that are not in their best interests and may need more direction about what to do differently.

This leads to the idea that people have basic needs that must be met in order for them to be satisfied, content, and balanced. In Sandra's case, she may be satisfied with how she is spending her time, but she is neglecting several basic needs, and over time, this will affect her well-being. When Dr. Christiansen and I reviewed all the work of researchers who examined the qualities of a good life, we came up with four basic needs that seem to be common in most of the research.[5] People need to engage in activities that accomplish the following:

1. Contribute to a healthy body: This means activities like getting adequate sleep, eating well, exercising, and managing your medical needs.
2. Support positive and self-affirming relationships: We do things with people we care about and who care about us.
3. Remain challenging and interesting to them: At least some activities need to engage us in challenging ways. Granted, many important everyday activities are not challenging or interesting, like commuting, paying bills, or cleaning.
4. Contribute to their positive identity: These activities help us fulfill important roles and be the people we want to be. For

example, caregiving, doing housework, or volunteering may not be challenging, but they are important.

It's not just matching what we do and want to do. It is also about making sure that these four important needs are met through our activity choices. Sandra seems to be meeting her need for challenge and interest through her work, but she is lacking in activities that support her healthy body and her relationships. She may be partially contributing to a positive identity through work but lacking in her other important roles. Sandra is not creating a balanced life according to the LBM.

In my research, I had 458 people with a demographic profile approximate to the US population (gender, age, race, income, and education) complete surveys about life balance, stress, well-being, and need satisfaction. As it turns out, both matching what we do and want to do and meeting the four needs are important for a balanced life, and these were significantly associated with lower stress, higher well-being, and need satisfaction.[31] Interestingly the groups who looked the worse—that is, those who had lower life balance, higher stress, lower well-being, and need satisfaction—were women with children at home, people working full time, and people of color.

In another study with 1,048 people, I found a profile of those with the best life balance scores and the lowest stress scores. It won't be a surprise. The most balanced people were white men over sixty-one years or older who had earned a master's degree. They had incomes between $81,000 and $100,000. They lived in the suburbs and had two children, but the children were not at home. Most were not working. But if they were working, they were self-employed. They owned a home and lived in the United States.[32]

The finding that certain expected characteristics predictably related to life balance reinforces the last main idea in the LBM, that is, the environment in which we live can create supports or barriers to life balance. Not every choice of activities is within our control. Women with children at home cannot abandon their children to engage in a pleasurable or challenging activity. People who work full time do so out of necessity, and it uses up a large chunk of their allotted twenty-four hours. People of color may have other environmental barriers that were reflected in their lower life balance scores. Chapter 9 will discuss this in much more detail.

Knowing that life doesn't always go as planned—that is, we cannot always spend time the way we want to, and many events are simply out of our control—makes it even more important to pay attention and identify places where we need to make some adjustments when possible. That's where the skill comes in and will be reinforced throughout this book. I am constantly aware of matching desired to actual time spend in activities, and I regularly take stock of whether or not I am meeting my four needs. When there is a gap, I try to find an answer, and although I'm not always successful in achieving the match, I keep trying, and I know the goal.

Life Balance Inventory (LBI)

How are you doing in terms of finding the match between actual and desired activities in each of the four need areas? Are you attending to your health needs? Have you spent the amount of time you want doing things with people you care about? Are you bored? Or have you included at least some challenging activities into your life? Finally are you doing things that reflect the person you want to be? You should be asking yourself these questions on a regular basis, and once you find a weak area, make some choices that will improve the situation.

If you are interested in a more in-depth exploration of your life balance, you can go to this link http://minerva.stkate.edu/lbi.nsf and take the life balance inventory (LBI) that I developed to measure the constructs in the LBM. It is a fifty-three-item survey where you determine if the time you spend in activities is one of the following: about right for you, sometimes too much or too little, or always too much or too little. You will get an overall score that says how well you found the match between desired and actual activities in your life. It will also show how well you are doing with the match in each of the four need areas. The LBI has been tested scientifically for its properties of reliability and validity, and it is a good tool for measuring life balance.[33]

Maddie

"Life balance means to maintain peace and tranquility in life." According to Maddie, the way to maintain peace and tranquility in life is to attend to one's needs without being overloaded in any area. Maddie's identified needs match the health, relationship, challenge, and identity needs of the LBM described in this chapter. She quickly came to an answer when asked what life balance meant to her. She first identified spirituality as the source of meaning in her life and deeply embedded in her identity. Her relationships, especially her husband of forty-seven years, her four adult children, and their families, are absolute priorities, and she admits they always come first in her daily activity choices. She added, "Of course I try to maintain my health through exercise and good nutrition, and I need to do some things that are fun and challenging."

The biggest challenge Maddie faces is that she has multiple sclerosis (MS), a progressive neurological disease that interferes with her sensory and motor systems. The only treatment of MS is to manage the symptoms and attempt to slow the progression of the disease. Maddie was diagnosed at age eighteen when she noticed numbness, tingling, and weakness on one side of her body. One of the most disabling symptoms of MS is fatigue, and Maddie explained, in order to manage fatigue, she has to plan her days and rest many times during her daily activities. Maddie also manages depression, another symptom of MS and side effect of her medications. Her only visible symptom of MS is a slight leg drag when she walks.

When Maddie was a young mother, the treatment options for MS were far inferior to now. Those years were often very difficult because, when she had a flare-up of weakness and numbness, the treatment option was medication to reduce inflammation, which had

its own complications. And results were only moderate. Maddie was determined to care for her family first, but the flare-up of fatigue, depression, and physical symptoms made it difficult. Her life balance journey was probably the lowest at that time, but when she looks back, she sees how those life experiences have made her a more patient, accepting, and empathetic person. So much was out of her control that her only healthy option was to learn to accept one day at a time, find meaning in everyday things, and be grateful for what she had.

Maddie shared a story about a time when she was feeling imbalanced with all of her limited energy devoted to her family and symptom management, leaving little energy left for personal fulfillment. She signed up for guitar lessons that eventually led to playing in the church choir, followed by her husband joining in the choir and a lifetime of sharing music with others. This single choice opened up a spiritual calling that continues to bring meaning to Maddie's life.

In most of the stories in this book, you'll hear about how important it is to make plans and to make deliberate, strategic choices for improving life balance. Maddie has learned to not depend on plans. She admits to once being a planner, being very organized with consistent routines for getting things done, like cleaning the whole house every week. Now she still makes plans because she wants things to look forward to, but she has mastered the art of taking each day as it comes, knowing she may have to make adaptations because of her health. Her standards for things like a clean house have changed, and now she makes activity choices that take care of her health first. Maddie's ability to let go of expectations took years of practice, and she believes, now at age sixty-six years, she lives a balanced life. For example:

- Health needs: She is on a new regiment of treatment for MS that involves daily shots intended to slow the progression

of the disease. Her symptoms have definitely plateaued in the past several years. She loves to ride a bike but can no longer ride a standard bike because of frequent falls, so she purchased a recumbent bike that she enjoys just as much. She willingly participates in activities that require walking but lets her companions know she will need to pace herself and take frequent sit breaks.

- Relationship needs: Maddie continues to be completely devoted to her family, which has grown to include thirteen grandchildren. She prioritizes time with them and tries to be available when needed. She and her husband have a motor home and belong to a travel club, where she enjoys the company of other retired friends.

- Challenge needs: Even though Maddie can't always count on having energy for physical activities, she has her hobby of card making that she can do anytime. Card making stirs her creative and spiritual selves when she makes inspirational cards for any occasion. This passion has grown to where she sells them in craft shows and fosters rewarding social connections with other card makers.

- Identity needs: One challenge for people who have a chronic disease is to not let the disease define who they are. Sometimes managing a disease can be so all-encompassing that there is little left of one's true self. Maddie has learned to put her MS in the background and deal with her symptoms as needed but to create a meaningful life unrelated to her disease. She places her spirituality at her center and focuses on being grateful for everyone and everything in her life. Maddie values all her roles and feels most fulfilled when she can be there for the people she loves.

MS is a progressive disease. Maddie knows, even though she has stayed fairly stable over the past few years, her symptoms could get worse. She admits that her positive attitude has to be nurtured because it is easy to start worrying about what could happen in the future. Her plans for the future are to continue to travel in the motor home, spend more time with her children and grandchildren, care for her elderly mother, and continue exercising and card making.

I asked her what the readers can learn from her about life balance, and she said, "Know that life can be challenging with MS, but you can overcome the challenges with a positive attitude. Look toward the things you can do and not at the things you cannot do."

PART 2

THE FIVE KEY AGREEMENTS ABOUT LIFE BALANCE

CHAPTER 5

It Is a Journey, Not a Destination

So far I have not found a single person who will admit to living a balanced life. There are likely some days or weeks when everything lines up and you feel a deep sense of contentment, peace, and balance. Other times you are busy with your life, not necessarily feeling balanced but not feeling terribly dissatisfied either. When things are crazy busy or a series of negative events topples on you at once, you just grit your teeth and get through it, hoping to regain some semblance of peace when it is over. This ebb and flow in life is more normal than having a balanced life.

A good metaphor for the journey is a highway (your life trajectory) with the center of the road representing perfect life balance. In the LBM described in chapter 4, we must meet our needs for physical health, satisfying relationships, challenge, and the creation of a positive identity. Imagine each of these needs as a car going down the freeway, and when one of those needs is met through your daily activities, the car representing that need drives down the center of the road. If you met all four of those needs at all times throughout your life, your four cars would be driving down the center of the highway without any errors. I don't know of anyone who has such a perfect driving record or exemplary life for that matter.

Instead at any given time in your life, you may have some cars on the road and others off. Let's imagine your relationships car is going down the center of the road, but your other vehicles are driving in the ditch or have completely taken a wrong turn. In other words, you are not meeting your needs for physical health, challenge, or positive identity through your patterns of activity. The main idea for creating a balanced life is to recognize when you are off the road and steer it back. For the wrong turns, it may take longer to get back on the road, but once you are in the ditch, it may only take a slight lifestyle adjustment to get back on the road. You can view your life balance journey by looking back on the road you've traveled for the tracks your cars have made. What percentage of your life was spent off the road? Which cars were most problematic? How often did you pay attention to your cars and make the needed adjustments?

The way you meet your needs will be different in various life stages. Keeping the cars on the road may become more or less challenging as life changes. If you are a young adult, you may be consumed with your future, including finishing school, determining a career, finding a partner, or establishing a family. Recent census data in the United States shows that this period is lasting longer than it did a few decades ago. Young adults are delaying decisions about marriage and life partners, childbearing, and work until they are in their thirties. This delay may mean young adults are much more ready for the next stages or just reflect the complexities of establishing themselves socially and financially in this culture. During this period, change is constant, and feeling balanced may depend on how much progress is being made toward goals, satisfaction with relationships, or career trajectories. As you can imagine, this can be a bumpy road, and feeling balanced could vary from day to day.

Sarah is sixty-two years old and reflecting back on her journey. After graduating from college and working two years as a social worker, she married Gerry when she was twenty-four years old. They rented an apartment, and Sarah remembers loving this stage, going headlong into cooking and decorating the apartment. They were trying to save money for a house so Sarah's challenge was to find nice used furniture that she could refinish and fix up. She made the curtains and had fun creating art for the walls out of scrap wood and metal. Luckily Sarah had an artistic flair, and the things she made looked really great. It was easy to feel balanced because she and Gerry had similar work schedules and had every evening and weekend to do what they wanted. She was happy in her relationships, felt challenged with her projects and work, loved her identity as wife, and remained physically active. All her cars were driving down the center of the road. Then at age twenty-seven, she had the first of four children.

Life can change quite dramatically with the arrival of children. Data from the American Time Use Survey show adults living in households with children under age six spent an average of two hours per day providing direct childcare, such as taking care of their physical needs, reading, or interacting with them. In contrast, when their children were older, between ages six and seventeen years, they spent less than half as much time providing direct childcare, about forty-nine minutes per day.[34]

Young parents' lives are generally focused on getting by from day to day and getting all the basic chores done while managing demands of jobs and taking care of their children's needs. Even when parents are engaging in leisure activities or household chores, they are multitasking with childcare. Adults spend an average of five to six hours per day providing secondary childcare, that is, they had at least one child in their care while doing activities other than direct childcare.[34]

Women spend more time on average providing childcare than men do. In the end, adults with young children have less time available for meeting their own needs. Although this may seem like an argument for chronic imbalance in a young parent's life, my LBM would suggest that the parents might not be meeting all their needs but may be meeting their identity need, being a good parent for children they love. Then it is a matter of making small adjustments to make sure they squeeze in some activities that meet their other needs.

Parenting young children can be very satisfying and meaningful and contribute to life balance. Maybe you can relate to those wonderful but often rare moments when everyone in the family is in sync and enjoying something together. We found those moments when we were camping. When everyone was fed, rested, and happy around the campfire at night, I would swell with pride and satisfaction, feeling grateful and contented, and if someone asked me, I would say I was balanced. Then of course, driving home with fighting in the backseat and complaints of boredom and hunger, the sense of balance would be over.

Sarah remembers feeling very fulfilled because being a mother was meaningful to her, and of course, she loved her family. She stayed at home to care for them until the youngest went to kindergarten. During those years Sarah went headlong into motherhood and domesticity and loved most of it. She tried to involve her children in lots of community activities. She enjoyed baking, and of course, keeping the house clean involved constant work. To keep from feeling isolated, she found friendship in a church group of mothers who met once a week to do activities together. Generally Sarah would say these were great years, but she put a few things on the back burner because they were no longer priorities or simply too much hassle to add to her life. She found it difficult to exercise regularly because she couldn't leave the house without someone watching the kids. She worked it out with Gerry, but it added a layer of complication and sometimes didn't feel worth the effort. The kids were usually up at dawn, and she never felt like she had enough sleep. She still tried to sew, do crafts, and decorate their new house, but the constant interruptions and mess took away some of the luster. And she didn't do it as much as she used to.

In this stage Sarah needed to rethink how she would meet her needs. She felt good about her relationships, and she felt proud of her identity as a good mother, homemaker, and wife. She tried not to worry about her career because this stage was a temporary step-out, but sometimes she felt bored at home and out of sync with her career-oriented friends. The vehicles off the road were her health and challenge cars.

Over time our views of what we want our lives to look like may change. What Sarah found satisfying and fulfilling in her early marriage and parenting years began to change, and she was looking for new challenges given the changing dynamics in her family.

Midlife can be consumed with many new challenges like raising teenagers, caring for aging parents, adjusting to divorce, managing health issues, building a career, and any number of changes. Some would say this period is hardest to find balance because of the increased complexity of home and work life. Teenagers no longer are predictably at the family events or in bed at a reasonable hour so you can do your thing in the evening. By their nature, teenagers are seeking independence and autonomy from their parents, setting up many potential power struggles that are stressful for everyone.

Additionally many midlife adults are taking care of their aging parents. Because they are sandwiched between caring for children and parents, this group has been coined "the sandwich generation." The National Alliance of Caregiving and AARP queried 6,806 American households and reported that 31.2 percent reported at least one person in the household had served as an unpaid family caregiver in the past twelve months and about 5.5 percent are caring for an older adult and their own children simultaneously.[35]

Caregivers average forty-eight years old, approximately the age when career opportunities are more available due to accumulated work experience, yet work must be balanced with the reported average of twenty hours per week of caregiving responsibilities. The time crunch sets up a perfect storm for stress during midlife, and it is easy to see how relationships could deteriorate, and health issues could arise. So 31 percent of caregivers report high stress, and half of caregivers (53 percent) say that their caregiving takes time away from friends and other family members. Those who have sacrificed this time with family and friends are far more likely to feel high emotional stress (47 percent) than are those who have been able to maintain the time they spend with family and friends (14 percent).[35]

Clearly midlife years can be very different among people depending on their life circumstances. In the best of scenarios, however, midlife can be a time when you achieve significant life goals, and you are able to contribute more to the community and increase your social activities. These activities are more attractive and available in midlife because of accumulated experience, more time unrelated to childcare, and an increased attention to the welfare of others. Interestingly a large percentage of people in midlife reported peak experiences involving interpersonal joy. Others reported peak experience related to achievement in life or career.[36]

Additionally midlife may also be a time when relationships are most satisfying and meaningful. Recent neurological research has shown that people in midlife have a greater capacity for loving relationships and life satisfaction than people in other developmental stages do. This greater capacity for love may be attributable to changes in brain functioning, as neurological studies have found that skills associated with empathy, verbal memory, and the ability to see connections and relationships among various elements all increase from young adulthood to midlife.[37]

Sarah felt like she had two major midlife stages, early midlife and late midlife. In early midlife, she was busier than ever. She went back to work full time as a social worker for at-risk older adults. Her work was very rewarding, and she was constantly problem-solving and being creative when finding solutions for her clients. She felt constantly stimulated and no longer needed the creativity of crafts and cooking because her challenge car was in the center of the road. With teenagers and young adult children, family events were constant, like graduations, weddings, and sporting and school-related events. Basically between her job and children, her life was scheduled for her, and she was generally happy. The one need that was not met, however, was her health. Because of the pace of life, Sarah found it difficult to exercise regularly, and she found herself eating on the run a lot. She gained twenty pounds during this period and was struggling with the symptoms of menopause.

Suddenly it seemed to Sarah that the race was over. She described this as her current stage, late midlife. She is still working but plans to retire in about three years, mostly because of pressure from her husband. She is at the top of her career as a manager of the department, but the challenges that used to stimulate her now feel repetitive and fatiguing. Her children are all out of the house and living independently, both of her parents died, and her husband, who is retired, is managing most of the housework. Now time is abundant, and she is struggling with how to fill it. Even though she has not lost weight, she feels better about her health because the one thing she did was join a fitness center that she attends at least twice a week. Sarah admits to feeling lost because work is no longer as stimulating, and she is bored with all her time off. How will she ever retire? In this stage, Sarah's challenge car took a wrong turn, and she is trying to find new activities that will challenge and interest her, especially during retirement.

Retirement should be a time to experience life balance because you can finally do what you want to do. Research on the LBM showed that indeed people who were not working and men over age sixty-one reported the most life balance and least amount of stress. Swedish researchers followed people before, during, and after retirement and found that the main determinant of whether they were able to achieve positive life experiences as retirees was the presence or absence of social, physical, and enjoyable activities in their lives.[38]

Retirees were most satisfied with their lives if they were able to do the things they wanted to do and had a satisfactory variety and if activities had the following characteristics:[39]

- Self-determination: They felt in control of their leisure choices.
- Competence: They felt their skill matched the demands of the activity.
- Challenge: Experiences stretched their limits and provided novel stimuli.

Of the three characteristics, experiencing challenge had the most power for life satisfaction. But with retirement, suddenly the challenge and social contacts that work provided are gone, and unless there is a good substitute, retirement can be a difficult adjustment.[38]

Researchers found that retirement wasn't total bliss and felt more complex and unpredictable than imagined. For example, retirees found it difficult to create satisfying routines without the external demands imposed by work. Without the expectation to be somewhere at a certain time, it is understandable that routines like breakfast and getting ready in the morning can be prolonged without consequence. Retirees were surprised they didn't take up new activities as expected. In fact, research has shown that typically most people do not take up new activities after retirement but do more of the familiar activities. There are always exceptions. The best adaptation to retirement was making the least amount of changes.[40] The meaning of some activities changed when work was not there. There is nothing better than relaxing at the cabin for a weekend following a busy and stressful workweek. But when there was no contrast, nothing to relax from then, the weekend at the cabin lost some of its meaning.

On the other hand, if you ask retirees how they like it, you'll hear things like, "I've never been busier … I don't know how I ever had time to work … I love the freedom to do what I want to do." So clearly retirement is generally a positive thing.

I came to the conclusion in my work that we need to prepare to retire, not just financially, but actually prepare our lifestyles. Sarah is doing that now. She is starting to experiment with volunteer opportunities, checking out potential retirement communities for the winter months, and exploring a phased retirement plan with her employer. She is taking a community education class on scrapbooking, hoping that might stir a new hobby for her.

Amanda

Life balance is "being happy and satisfied in the main areas of life: home and work. To not be bored and to be motivated in all areas I care about." According to my research, working women with children at home are more stressed and have poorer life balance than other groups do. Amanda represents that group. She is thirty-five years old and married with three children under the age of seven years. She is a principle scientist for a medical engineering company. Amanda describes herself as a goal setter and goal achiever. Right out of her graduation from college with a physics degree, she immediately enrolled in a graduate program for biomedical engineering. Why? She said, "I wanted to get it out of the way so I could have a family."

She married Mark, and over the first few years, she focused on finishing her education. Amanda reflected back on that period as being rather stress-free but not because she wasn't busy. Her schedule allowed her time to do things she enjoyed, like run, play soccer, and socialize with friends and family. Her husband was supportive, and she could totally focus on becoming the person she wanted to be, physically, intellectually, and emotionally. At the time she probably didn't appreciate how much "me time" she enjoyed because everything she did was achieving a goal she set for herself. Balance at that time in Amanda's life looked really busy from an outsider's view, but that lifestyle was rewarding and happy. Goal achieved. She received her PhD in biomedical engineering. She was physically fit. She had a fulfilling marriage and stayed in touch with her family and friends.

The thing about goal-setters is that there is always a new goal out there. All of her early married years were setting her up for the next stage of being a mother. She didn't have a goal of being a mother of twins, but that is what happened. Amanda admits she has a very

modern marriage where there is no traditional allocation of roles, and without her husband's cooperation, it might have been a different story.

Interestingly Amanda felt, with two parents, it was manageable caring for the twins. Each parent took one baby, and life was pretty good. Note here that Amanda's idea of a pretty good life changed significantly from even one year earlier, where she could run, go out, or do whatever she needed for fulfillment. During infant stages, getting enough sleep was all she needed to feel balanced.

When the twins were three months old, she was forced to return to full-time work at the medical engineering company where she was employed. This stood out as a major time of stress in her life, full of guilt about leaving her twins and everyday exhaustion in working and caring for the babies. When Amanda discussed this time of her life, the major focus was on trying to find balance between work and home, and she advocated for herself to negotiate a four-day workweek. She started with four ten-hour days and was eventually able to negotiate four eight-hour days with every Monday off.

Amanda continued to work four days a week when her third child was born and the twins were two years old. Looking back, Amanda admits this was the most difficult period. With three children, one parent tended to the twins while the other tended to the newborn. Therefore, instead of doing everything together, as happened with the twins, now the family unity was split, at least until their third child was about a year old. They experienced lots of stress and exhaustion, but Amanda sees her Mondays off as the pressure release valve where she can recharge, be with her children, and be the mother she wants to be. She views this day off as the key to her life balance. Mondays off allow her to have a relaxing morning with the kids and time to give them her attention. On Mondays she likes to cook a meal where they can sit down together as a family with leftovers for the week. She tries to use her Mondays to volunteer at

school or be present for the twins' activities. "Me time" has been reduced significantly, and although she tries to dabble in exercise, music, and knitting when possible, generally they only happen when everything else is taken care of. This seems to be fine for now because Amanda shifted her priorities to being a mother and wife, and "me time" can come later.

Choosing time with her children and reducing her workload came at a price, however. She feels like she has to work harder than her peers do to be seen as valuable to the company. She has to be very focused and productive at all times to prove to her company that she can do a full-time job in four days. She also sees peers being recognized and earning promotions, and although she accepts her choice to take a slower pace, she sometimes worries it will affect her career.

Amanda's advice to young parents who are working outside of the home is to choose their priorities so they don't regret it later. If they want to be at home more, then advocate for themselves. She was the first woman scientist in her group to request a four-day workweek, and it took persistence on her part to get it approved. "Don't be afraid to ask," she advises. She also has mentors who support her choice and have demonstrated that taking a different path did not hold back their careers in the long run. She suggests finding other people in similar circumstances who understand your story. In her case, other mothers of twins were extremely helpful listeners and made her feel less alone.

Another crossroad for life balance is ahead for Amanda. Her youngest child will be going to kindergarten in another year, and she feels like there is no reason for her to have Mondays off if everyone is in school. She is preparing to go back to a five-day workweek, but it was clear in the interview that she already grieves the loss of home time and finds the decision difficult. Her next challenge is to negotiate the best possible schedule that meets her employer's needs and lets her live true to her values and priorities.

CHAPTER 6

It Requires Doing Things

When the neurologist confirmed the diagnosis of MS, Paul was sure his life would come crashing down. His wife and two kids would leave him, he'd lose his job, and he would no longer have any enjoyable activities in his life. Instead, to his relief, his symptoms got better, and he continued to work as an instructional technology professional at a community college. His leg would occasionally feel numb, and once in a while, he felt overly tired, but he was generally able to lead the life he wanted. Paul loves volunteering at his church and going to musical events, and he has a regular poker club with some of his buddies of over thirty years. He was pleasantly surprised that he was managing so well and assumed he would continue to beat the odds into old age. Overall he was meeting his needs in the following:

- Health: although he did want to exercise more than he is currently doing.
- Relationships: He had longtime friends, a loving wife, and children.
- Challenge: He was constantly creating and problem-solving in his job.
- Identity: He was pleased that his disease did not define him.

Things did come crashing down about seventeen years later, however, when he had a flare-up of the disease that never returned to normal. Suddenly both legs lost strength, and his right arm went in and out of numbness. He had to take an earlier-than-planned retirement at age sixty because of severe fatigue and had new problems with memory and concentration. By the time he was sixty-five years old, he had difficulty walking more than a few feet and used a scooter to get around the community. At home he got around by holding onto the furniture and walls.

Paul was devastated. His life, as he knew it was over, and he didn't know how to get it back. He reacted by closing in on himself, staying home, and giving up on his interests. His wife has been pushing him to have a positive attitude and to be more accepting of his life. But he was not doing anything that was meeting his needs for life balance. All his cars were driving off the road.

Paul learned the hard way that, when his health was good, he simply went about his daily activities without any thought of their importance to well-being. For example, he woke up, groomed, dressed, ate, took out the garbage, and made his lunch. Those activities were simply preparatory to what he cared about, his job, and his family or social activities. They were so automatic and part of his habits that he did not even remember much about doing them. But once his MS symptoms restricted him from doing some of the things he took for granted, small things like taking out the garbage became more important. He had to plan two hours every morning to bathe, dress, and groom himself, and by the time that was done, he was too tired to do anything else. Paul felt, if he had difficulty with basic self-care activities, he shouldn't be able to engage in the other things that brought him joy, like music, socialization, and volunteering.

Paul was taking medication to reduce some of the MS symptoms and improve his health, but he would not be well until he began to participate in life again. His poker buddies, all retired, changed the time of the game to mid-afternoon because Paul was less fatigued then. They also held the games in homes that were accessible to his scooter. The church found volunteer activities that he could do from his scooter, like preparing mailings and updating the website. Finally Paul's adult children gave him season tickets to symphony hall concerts. Although he was doing things in different ways, he began living again.

You have to do it. Doing is part of our human condition. As humans we have a natural drive for action and engaging with the world. You will not have a balanced life by wishing, dreaming, or imagining one. You have to do the things that are meaningful to you and meet your needs.

This doing has more science behind it than you may be aware. Occupational science (doing science) is the science of everyday living, and several universities offer advanced degrees in the discipline. Several professional journals publish occupational science research. This science explores occupations, which are "the ordinary and familiar things that people do every day"[41] and how they impact our health and well-being. You probably use a different term than "occupations," like activities, tasks, actions, or engagement, but the important part is the doing. Occupational science has helped occupational therapists and other scientists understand the value of occupation to health and well-being, and my hope is that this book will also help you appreciate the significance of doing.

The profession of occupational therapy was built on the importance of doing, emerging from the influence of the mental hygiene and the moral treatment movements in the early twentieth century. Prior to these movements, people with mental illnesses, people who were disabled, or people who were significantly different from the norm were living in asylums with deplorable and inhuman conditions. They were confined, restrained, or simply ignored and given only basic physiologic necessities such as food, drink, and toilet. There were no social opportunities, and they were kept out of sight of the general population. The early philosophy of occupational therapy was that these people were worthy of care and needed to have opportunities for normalcy, like being able to participate in everyday activities. Simple routines like dressing, dishing up food, taking a shower, or playing a game of catch were awe-inspiring if never done before. In fact it turned out to be a key component in healing and restoration of health. The introduction of humane treatment and engagement in activities changed lives and began the eventual integration of people with mental illness and disabilities into society.

Another major influence supporting the importance of doing was the arts and crafts movement that emerged in the late 1900s. This movement responded to a perceived dehumanization resulting from industrialization. The crowding, noise, and repetitive physical demands of factory work was seen as a contributor to mental and physical illness. Arts and crafts were viewed as a way to engage the mind and body in moral and curative ways. In other words, through these activities, people struggling with mental or physical illness were able to heal or restore as their creativity and skills expressed themselves. For example, once a person is depressed and feels hopeless, he or she may get a sense of pride and self-esteem upon completion of a hand-built and nicely painted birdhouse. Likewise, if someone had a physical limitation, such as loss of an arm, being able to complete a one-handed weaving would instill a sense of accomplishment and hope for the future.

After WWI, scores of men who had serious injuries that resulted in amputations, blindness, and permanent nerve damage were returning home. Occupational therapists used their underlying value of doing to provide rehabilitation services to injured or disabled veterans who were unable to continue doing what they needed or wanted to do. For example, when the loss of lower limbs resulted in life from a wheelchair, they needed to find adaptations so they could continue to drive, work, play, and care for themselves and others from a seated position.

The deep-rooted value of doing was a completely new paradigm for the medical world. Until recently the contribution of occupational therapy was appreciated, but considered soft or extra with the hard sciences of bio physiology or neurology viewed as the only legitimate contribution to disease management. People were considered an accumulation of various biological systems or organs that interacted with each other, like the lungs and heart. When there was a problem in one of the systems, the approach was to find the bio physiological cause and fix it. Of course, over time, it became clear that there were many other reasons for poor health that couldn't always be fixed medically. So scientists began looking at people more holistically to understand their lifestyles and the big picture of their health concerns.

For example, obesity rates continue to climb in the United States with more than one in three adults considered obese.[42] Medical professionals alone are unable to adequately help people with this health concern because they can't fix the complex lifestyle and behavioral habits associated with obesity. I did a recent study of 2,338 participants between the ages of eighteen and forty-nine years and found that those who were obese reported significantly lower life balance and higher stress compared to people who were not obese.[43]

Does stress and inactivity lead to obesity? Or is it the other way around where obesity limits the activities people engage in and increases stress? It's probably a combination of both. The bottom line is that doing and obesity are related. Changing habits and routines associated with sedentary lives and overeating may go a long way toward weight loss that attending to caloric intake alone cannot accomplish.

The value of doing is recently accepted as important to health on a global scale. The World Health Organization (WHO) used to define health as the absence of disease, but now includes the ability to fully participate in life, to do what we need and want to do in our lives.[44] So if you have a chronic disease, such as diabetes, but are able to fully participate in life as you desire, you would be described as healthy with a disease to manage. On the other hand, if you do not have any disease or illness but have a desire but cannot find employment because of economic, social, political, or cultural barriers, you do not live a healthy life.

Are you satisfied with your doing? You are probably familiar with the difficulty in actually following through on the things you said or thought you were going to do. How many times have you said you were going to take time to play an instrument, put aside time for your art or craft interests, or begin an academic program of study but found it too hard to fit into your life on a regular basis? How about that promise to yourself to keep up with your friends and to go out more often? Maybe you were going to be more consistent in attending religious services or to be more engaged in the church activities. Insert your particular wish, and you can probably relate to this.

The main message from this chapter is you have to actually do it, and then the rewards follow. Your lifestyle consists of the everyday things you do from day to day, week to week, and year to year. What do you need to continue doing, and what needs to be done differently for your balanced life?

Janice

Life balance is "going to bed every night with plans for things to do the next day." Janice has fully embraced the idea of doing as important to her life balance. She said her biggest barrier to doing was being single all of her life. She has a personality that is very open to new experiences, and she is happiest when she can have something fun and different to do every day and gets her out of the house. Because she lives alone, she has plenty of downtime, so her major drive in life is to be active with other people and attend art, theatre, music, cultural, culinary, and any other event happening in the city. Janice is sixty-one years old and just retired from the hospital system where she worked her entire adult life. After forty-one years, she left cold turkey. I was interested in how a sudden change from full-time work to retirement would feel to Janice.

The main theme that came out of her interview was a strong desire for flexibility. Flexibility is key for Janice because she loves to do things in the community but needs to be available when other people are available or she does them alone. This theme of flexibility threads through many of the major decisions she made throughout life. She decided to pursue a nursing degree for many reasons, but a major reason was because it would offer her more choices and flexibility in her lifestyle. Once she made this decision, she went headlong into courses while working full time and advocated for herself to get into nursing school. She looks back on two years of intensity with a contented acceptance because, even though she was outrageously busy, it was meaningful to her. She happily gave up other activities. This was a period of life balance because she was challenged, school was meaningful, and she was part of a social network with other adult students.

Once she started her nursing career, she found out quickly that there were some disappointments with the flexibility she expected. For several years she worked alternating shifts that made it very difficult to plan activities with other people. For example, if there was an evening event, she might have to leave early to go to work. Another unexpected barrier was managing her vacation time. Even though she had generous vacation benefits, planning had to occur once a year for the entire year. This was difficult for making plans with other people who typically don't plan so far in advance. If an opportunity to travel came up later in the year and she didn't ask for the time off, she missed out. Her lifestyle did not support making commitments, such as joining groups or clubs, because her schedule would often conflict and was not predictable from week to week. Additionally her natural personality was shy, and it took a lot of courage for her to join groups alone. Her personal reservations and unpredictable schedule tended to isolate her more than she wanted. Janice reports this period of shift work as a low point in her life balance, and she was determined to find a job with better hours.

She is persistent, however, and several years and applications later, she landed a job in primary care that gave her a consistent schedule and weekends off. This opened up more opportunities for life balance and broadening her social network. Once her schedule was more predictable, she needed to find more people available and interested in doing things. In this stage, against her natural personality, Janice forced herself to initiate activities with people, join a travel group, and find comfort in doing some things alone. This all led up to her recent past where she landed a gravy job because she was an experienced, seasoned nurse.

Janice put a lot of thought into whether she was ready to retire or not. Of course being financially ready was first, but once security was

established, her main planning revolved around what kind of a lifestyle she would have. There were two main drivers to her decision:

1. Even though she finally landed the perfect job, in short time, she found that it no longer challenged her.
2. Her definition of life balance is to end a day with upcoming plans, to always have something to look forward to. Of course, in order to be absolutely available, her schedule needed to be open.

I interviewed Janice about three months after she retired. She is currently looking for a living situation that requires little house or yard maintenance on her part so she has the flexibility to leave at any time without worrying. Looking back, she wonders if she should have pushed herself to be more involved with various groups for additional social capital to lean on in retirement. Now that she is completely flexible, however, she has rekindled friendships, reached out to others, joined groups, and volunteered in the neighborhood. Even if she has to participate in some activities alone, the doing keeps her balanced.

Activity: Daily Log of Activities

The first step in getting closer to life balance is to have a clear picture of what you are currently doing so you can see places in your day or week that have potential to be changed. This exercise will give you a good picture of your daily activities.

Choose a typical weekday for this exercise. Typical means there are not any special events going on that occur more sporadically, like a holiday, wedding, or graduation. Write down the following:

Time	What I was doing	How I felt
12:00 am		
1:00 am		
2:00 am		
3:00 am		
4:00 am		
5:00 am		
6:00 am		
7:00 am		
8:00 am		
9:00 am		
10:00 am		
11:00 am		
12:00 pm		
1:00 pm		
2:00 pm		
3:00 pm		
4:00 pm		
5:00 pm		
6:00 pm		
7:00 pm		
8:00 pm		
9:00 pm		
10:00 pm		
11:00 pm		

1. Examine your activities and how you felt. What were you doing that met the following needs: health, relationship, challenge, and identity?
2. Are you happy with the balance of need satisfaction in your daily activities? What were you doing that made you feel the best? The worst?
3. If you are not satisfied with the balance in your day, name one activity you would like to do more of or add to your day or week.
4. Where could you fit it in, and what activity would have to change in order for that to happen?

CHAPTER 7

It Is Good for You

We live in Minnesota, which means we are indoors four to five months out of a year. Everything is cold and dark during those months, and if you happen to be a person who enjoys gardening, tinkering in the garage, or doing woodwork, your options are limited. My husband Tom is one of those. He does not find enjoyment in long hours of reading, cooking, or playing video games that he could do indoors during the winter months. As I mentioned in the first chapter, we spent our first two and a half years living in a cabin in the woods. Imagine how dreadful winter could feel confined to a one-room cabin!

On the contrary Tom was generally pretty content, except for not finding a good job, because he was able to fill his days with a nice balance of rewarding and meaningful activities. Surviving in that primitive living situation required several hours of work each day. For example, he would snowshoe or ski into the woods to cut lumber for our wood stove, gather water, run a fur trap line, hunt, or go ice fishing, to name a few. Actually he mentioned several times that he could have been happy as a pioneer, homesteading like they did in the 1800s.

After our first child was born, we moved back to the Twin Cities, and suddenly Tom's options to do what he wanted to do in his free time were severely limited, primarily because we didn't have the right kind of space for his interests. We went through apartments and rented houses and then owned a small home. In the winter Tom would almost always have signs of seasonal affective disorder (winter blues) that were related to the fact that he was bored. His mind was not engrossed in an activity and allowed him too much time to focus on his dissatisfaction. We concluded over several years and multiple living situations that, when he was doing something like building a bookshelf, even in a crowded space, he was different. He was engaged, challenged, and motivated. The warmer seasons offered many more opportunities to do activities because he could work on equipment in the garage or outside and had plenty of gardening to keep him happy.

To cope with winter, we tried to stay active with outdoor activities, like cross-country skiing and snowshoeing, but as our family grew, it was almost impossible to do things as a family with an eight-year spread between developmental stages. Tom was keenly aware that he needed indoor projects to stay balanced, so over the years we bought woodworking tools like a table saw, jointer-planer, router, sander, and many hand tools so he could build furniture and keep his mind active. We lived in a split-entry home on a small lot with a two-car garage that we filled with our two vehicles and four claimed bedrooms. He had a ten-foot by ten-foot space in the laundry room for his hobbies, and he could take the cars out of the garage to use a larger space if needed. This was less than ideal because the garage was not heated, so he experimented with portable heaters. Even if the portable heaters helped, it was very difficult to get motivated to start a project in the cold garage with chunks of dirty ice from the cars on the floor. Most big woodworking projects took several days to complete, meaning both of our cars would be left outside in the cold and snow. The indoor space was fine for assembling, but once he sanded or applied finish, it was all over my laundry space.

Every winter I would beg Tom to get started on a project because I knew the difference it made in his mood and mental health, but it usually took several weeks for him to get motivated because of all the barriers. In the end the mess and inconvenience was worth it, and I have a house full of furniture.

We have both been convinced, to experience life balance, well-being, health, and quality of life, we needed to create lifestyles that allowed us to engage in meaningful activities and provided opportunities for challenging hobbies, especially during retirement. Tom retired early and wanted to live on a hobby farm. I still loved my job at the university in the middle of the city. I knew he needed more space for his hobbies to keep him vital during retirement, but I didn't want a long commute to work. We looked at houses and property for a couple of tough years, feeling like we did not have similar goals for our future. Luckily we found the perfect compromise with both of our lifestyles, keeping aging in place in mind. My commute is forty-five minutes, but it is worth it to come home to a one-level home with a brightly lit, heated, three-car garage on an acre of property that supports chickens. We have a large fenced-in vegetable garden and perennial gardens. There is even a large workshop in the basement that is well-lit, warm, and dry. We bought a lifestyle. Tom is blissfully trying to keep up with all the projects that need attention, and in the winter, he continues to build furniture, and he is getting pretty good at auto mechanics, to boot.

First, I'll state the obvious. Tom and I recognize the privilege of having good education and stable employment that allowed us to buy our new lifestyle. That's not available to everyone for any number of reasons, which will be the focus of chapter 9. Having said that, living a balanced life is good for you, and once your life impinges on that balance, you will not experience optimal well-being or health. Many things in life are out of our control, but the main point of Tom's story is that we need to be aware of what keeps us balanced and what activities are essential for our well-being and then try to create a lifestyle that includes them as best as we can.

The first thirty years of our life were far from ideal for Tom's life balance, but because we knew it was important, we deliberately tried to set up opportunities for him to engage in hobbies that kept him healthy during the dark and cold winter months. Even if we were unable to move to a more ideal situation, he was healthier and happier with the small modification we made than if we did nothing at all.

What was it about Tom's engagement in an activity that was so healthy? He would go into a state of flow when he was working on a project. Mihaly Csikszentmihalyi, a renowned psychologist who examined the science behind what makes life worth living and secrets to happiness, researched this state extensively.[18] His research led to the creation of flow theory that gave doing an entirely new respect in the positive psychology scientific community. Flow is a state of heightened focus and immersion in activities such as art, play, and work. During this immersion, you are so engaged in what you are doing that time flies, you are using your skills to utmost, and you are not thinking about yourself, but you are enjoying the activity for its own sake.[19] People who frequently experience flow during their activities express pleasure and lasting satisfaction. The flow state has been associated with well-being, positive health, and quality of life. Can you think of a time when you were doing something and, before you knew it, three hours went by? Maybe you forgot to eat lunch. According to years of accumulated research, that flow state is really good for you.

Of course you don't have flow experiences all the time because you do many other activities for other reasons. Being challenged is one important need according to various theories of life balance, but you do other things that are not challenging but equally as important to a balanced life. Being able to do what you need or want to do, whether it is challenging or not, is so important to your well-being that I will go out on a limb and say, in some cases, it is as important as taking medication. You can go far in improving your health with medication, insulin, for example, if you have diabetes. Insulin can save your life, but it is not enough for your overall health and well-being if you are unable to create a lifestyle that meets your needs. If your blood sugar levels are within a healthy range but you are unhappy with your relationships, you cannot seem to get the motivation to pull yourself away from the TV, or you are unhappy in your employment, you are not balanced, and it may impact your diabetes management. Arguably improvements in those areas will go a long way to improve your health, as medication does.

Occupational science researchers tested this idea of whether being able to participate in valued activities would impact health and quality of life. In a tightly controlled research study with 361 older adults in an inner city, groups of participants were taught the importance of everyday occupations, or doing in ways that helped them adapt to challenges associated with aging.[45] They problem-solved ways to engage in valued activities even with age-related problems, for example, negotiating public transportation with a walker or cane or continuing to read with visual problems. The results showed that participants who continued to do things they valued, even with age-related difficulty, had better physical health, physical and social functioning, vitality, mental health, and life satisfaction than similar older adults who did not participate in the program. In fact those who did not participate showed declines in health over the testing period. Since then there have been follow-up studies showing the health-related benefits of participation in meaningful activities.[46]

My own research used the same type of intervention, but targeting older adults who lived alone in single homes and were at risk for isolation.[47] One of the biggest barriers for this group was that they could no longer drive and were completely dependent on others for their activities. We arranged transportation for them to attend our educational groups once a week. The group members problem-solved ways to stay engaged in activities they cared about, given their existing barriers. We practiced taking public transportation and found low-cost taxi resources for the neighborhood, to name a few. The groups were planned to end after eight weeks, but they became so meaningful to the members that we continued offering them with resources from local churches and help from students. My research team found important health-related improvements, but the significant learning for us was how important activities and socialization became when lives were narrowed with age and resources.

One eighty-eight-year-old woman in our study was so thrilled to have a reason to bake some cookies to bring to our group. Another participant said she started walking more and, in so doing, had more socialization with neighbors. Even something as simple as having a reason to groom and put on some nicer clothing when attending the group was viewed as a benefit of the program. Living a balanced life is good for us.

We all do many things that make up a balanced life: grooming, shopping, cooking, cleaning, working, and socializing. And of course we do most of these without notice. When we do these things, we typically know the cultural rules to follow, like how to dress for work, where to find items in a grocery store, or how to negotiate public transportation. Imagine how the meaning of simple activities would change if you found yourself in another culture with entirely different rules for these activities. Some immigrants to the United States, for example, need to completely alter their everyday doing when moving from a rural agricultural environment to the heart of a metropolitan area in another country. Not only do they have new cultural norms to adjust to, they have also lost a past identity and have a pileup of barriers facing them, like finances, language, and isolation.

Using in-depth interviews with thirteen immigrant women to the United States, researchers found that their adjustment was very difficult and altered all their doing because they had to learn to do things in different spaces at different times in different roles. And the meaning of what they were doing was changed. All of this threatened their sense of identity and feelings of competency. For some this could be enough stress to make them mentally or physically ill and unable to cope. Yet the immigrants in this study felt that the way they coped and eventually discovered new opportunities was by continuing to do, even when they felt inadequate for a while.[48]

You already know that exercising, eating nutritiously, getting adequate sleep, and avoiding smoking and substance abuse are part of a healthy lifestyle. These messages are hard to miss in the mass public health campaigns. However, that knowledge may or may not translate into healthy habits for you, but at least you know about them and probably try to include them or, at a minimum, feel guilty when they are ignored. This chapter may give you a renewed appreciation for doing as another important component of health and well-being. Engagement in meaningful, challenging, and social activities can be as important as anything.

Exercise

My husband Tom needed to participate in flow experiences to keep his mental health. At times the flow experiences were easier or harder to attain depending on the environment. Attention to these experiences is important because they are a big part of your overall life balance.

1. Describe your flow experiences. What were you doing?

2. How often are you able to do this flow activity?
   Daily_____ Weekly_____ Monthly _____
   Very inconstantly _____

3. Is the amount of time you engage in this flow activity adequate for you? If not, how often would you like to engage in it?

4. What supports your ability to do this flow activity?
   • The arrangement of the time, materials, and space
   • The setup for minimal interruptions
   • Your family's/friends' support of the activity
   • The product of the activity is valued/used

5. What barriers prevent you from doing the flow activity?
   • Time, resources, and space
   • Family/social obligations
   • Other

6. Examine your flow activity supports. How can you capitalize on these to allow you to engage in flow activities?

7. Examine your flow activity barriers. Take each barrier, and identify at least one potential strategy to minimize the barrier.
   • Barrier _____
     Strategy to minimize the barrier _____

- Barrier _____
  Strategy to minimize the barrier _____
- Barrier _____
  Strategy to minimize the barrier _____
- Barrier _____
  Strategy to minimize the barrier _____

Remember: it is healthy to engage in your flow activity. Keep in mind, when you are in flow, you are not attending to others or anything else in your environment. These activities should be engaged in with full support and understanding from your family or other social supports.

CHAPTER 8

It Is Different for Everyone

Donald and Brian just graduated from college with business degrees and were both recruited to the same technology business because they were at the top of their class. The main office was in Manhattan, New York, so they decided to share rent for the first year until they could afford their own place. The apartment was less than a mile from the office with lots of restaurants, theatres, and shops nearby. Central Park was only a ten-minute walk from their place, and Brian went there a lot to run or rollerblade. Donald liked to walk and watch the people playing with their dogs. The first year was exciting and new with lots of visits from friends and family who wanted to experience Manhattan. For the first year, they were both totally engrossed in learning their jobs and working long hours.

Brian seemed to thrive in New York and started hanging out with new friends who enjoyed the theatre and arts, and he started taking art classes. He also discovered that he liked to cook because most of the time he was the one who prepared the meals for Donald and himself. Manhattan offered such fun variety for his leisure pursuits that Brian could hardly fit them all in. He was totally happy, felt very lucky, and thrived in his work and social lives.

Something wasn't right for Donald, however. Although he loved his job, he could not seem to find activities he enjoyed in the big city, so he stayed home a lot and watched TV. He was lonely too because Brian was always out with friends or taking classes. Donald grew up doing lots of hunting and fishing with his father and brother, and although he flew home a couple times to join them, he really missed the regular opportunities to be in nature and pursue his hobbies. His family owns wooded property in northern Wisconsin, and he was planning to work the land to promote more wildlife habitat and plant fruit trees. Donald became increasingly depressed and felt very guilty about his dissatisfaction because, after all, he had a very coveted job in a prestigious company in an exciting city. Why couldn't he get a grip and enjoy this lifestyle? Donald's challenge car was on the road because his job was great, but everything else was veering into the ditch. His life did not match his desired identity, his relationships were sparse, and he was not taking care of his health.

The activities we do to create a balanced life will be different for everyone. It seems pretty intuitive that there can't be a prescription of the best way to live our lives. Brian met his needs and found complete satisfaction with the lifestyle that made Donald depressed and feel wanting. We cannot assume that everyone will appreciate the same things, enjoy identical activities, or meet their needs in the same ways. The common thread is that we need to meet our need, not that we have to do certain activities.

When I was dating my husband Tom, I participated in many of the activities that he loved, like ice fishing and bowhunting. I just went along. These seemed fun at the time, but looking back, it was because I enjoyed his company, not the activities themselves. Tom feels that ice fishing is a relaxing and peaceful experience where he can recharge and renew. I was generally bored silly and brought a book along to pass the time. After several years of marriage, I finally declared that I would rather stay home instead of fishing, and it felt like a betrayal. Now I find myself looking forward to Tom's hunting and fishing trips so I can do the things I want to do, uninterrupted. Both of us can renew, alone!

The idea that everyone has different preferences isn't new to scientists who study human behavior; nor is it new to you. You know this because of your observations and experiences with family members, friends, and acquaintances. Most likely you have someone close to you who has some interests that are very different from yours. Scientists have found support for certain broad personality types,[49] and each personality type relates to different activity preferences. The study of personality types has evolved over the years, and although there is still some disagreement, the existence of five broad personality types has some consistent empirical support.[50] These personality types include the extreme ranges between extraversion/introversion, agreeableness/hostility, conscientiousness/spontaneity, neuroticism/emotional stability, and openness/closedness to experience.

In an abbreviated explanation, extraversion refers to people who tend to have high energy and positive emotions and are highly social. Agreeableness refers to people who tend to be friendly, compassionate, and cooperative. Conscientiousness refers to people who tend to be efficient, organized, and dependable. Neuroticism refers to people who tend to be sensitive and nervous and frequently experience negative emotions. And openness to experience refers to people who tend to be inventive and curious and appreciate a variety of experiences. People are not locked into a single type of personality, but the categories are helpful for scientists to generally understand how personality tendencies relate to other behaviors.

Personality type was found to be highly related to TV viewing, cultural participation, and reading choices[51] as well as preferences for leisure activities, such as going to a cultural event, engaging in extreme sports, enjoying nature, or participating in social events. [52] Individuals with a wide range of personality traits play video games, but it is believed that they may do so for somewhat different reasons. Gaming can involve social, competitive, daredevil, or mastermind challenges that appeal differently to people.[53] Even the type of music you prefer to listen to is related to your personality type,[54] whether it is reflective and complex, intense and rebellious, upbeat and conventional, or energetic and rhythmic.

I assert that the things you like to do in and of themselves aren't important for a balanced life. Your personality type is not important for a balanced life either. What is important is that you match your activities with your natural values, interests, and drives, and once you engage in them, you are meeting your needs.

Couples might feel like they have to enjoy everything together in order to be compatible. Parents might be disappointed that their family is not close if a child doesn't enjoy certain family activities. These are common scenarios and the source of lots of discussion among friends when comparing notes. During these times of disappointment, it might be helpful to remember that everyone meets his or her needs through different activities, and it is not realistic to expect everyone to enjoy the same things. The challenge is to find the optimal balance of together activities and alone activities.

Not only is finding the right balance of activities different for everyone, it is different for us from day to day. Something that is enjoyable and relaxing one day might feel boring or stressful another. Take a routine activity like cooking as an illustration. You have your own feelings about cooking, but those feelings may vary depending on the circumstances. If you are working full time and rush home to a hungry family, cooking may feel stressful and burdensome when you really just want to rest and unwind. On the other hand, it may be important for your identity to be a good parent, so you feel satisfied that you're fulfilling a role and the burden is worth it.

Of course there are other days when family members are uncooperative or unappreciative, and you resent having to cook. You may have an entirely different experience when cooking with friends for a dinner gathering. In this case, it becomes a restful, social, and highly engaging activity. Maybe you enjoy baking cookies with your kids. In that case, the measuring, breaking eggs, dumping flour into bowl, mixing, and scooping out dough are educational and skill-developing for your children, and you appreciate the bonding that occurs as well.

Cooking can be an entirely different experience from day to day and will meet different needs depending on the situation. Cooking can meet any of the following needs:

- Health: when you are preparing a nutritious meal
- Relationships: when you cook with others
- Identity: when you are cooking to care for your family
- Challenge: when you are trying out a new, complicated recipe

A good exercise might be to pay attention to what you're doing once in a while and reflect back on the activities in your day. When you engaged in those activities, what need did they satisfy, if any? For example, what did you do today that challenged you? What social connection did you make that strengthened relationships? How did you take care of your health? Did you do anything that contributed positively to the person you want to be?

Matthew and Megan

Life balance "is living out your priorities in a way that is best for your individual physical, emotional, and mental health." Matthew and Megan have been married for ten years and made a conscious decision to not have children. They both agreed that the primary reason was because it was never an internal drive. It didn't feel right to them, and they resisted being pressured to have kids just to be like everyone else. Megan worried, if she made a decision against her natural tendency, she couldn't take that decision back once children were in the picture. More importantly, they didn't have the desire for a lifestyle that children would create. They also value flexibility and want to be able to pursue their interests of travel, theatre, music, and animal care. This feels like the right choice to them, but they feel judged by others and feel like they have to justify this life choice.

The decision to not have children was difficult. For women in particular, the role of mother is so revered that Megan struggles with questions such as "Who am I as a woman, if not a mother?" "Will I regret this later?" and "What does my future look like?" She feels a sense of not being good enough as a woman, an outcast, someone who is viewed as unable to relate to when she is with her peers who are mothers. She feels a strong sense that she needs to be and/or do other amazing things to justify her decision not to have children. It is less of a problem for Matthew, perhaps because men are less tied to the role of father in social situations. He isn't exactly sure why it is less of a problem for him, but he is very aware that Megan struggles with it. Megan tearfully admits that her friendships change when children arrive, and once she finds out a friend is pregnant, she silently mourns. With each child born, she challenges her identity and life roles. Often when she gets together with her friends, they bring their

children and are naturally distracted by them, changing the course of their interactions. When this occurs, she is overpowered with an empty feeling because it is harder to connect in a meaningful way. Matthew also finds it more difficult to relate to friends who are parents because often their conversations go to their parenting experiences. Of course parents also have less flexibility, and it has become increasingly difficult to arrange activities together. Even though Matthew and Meghan understand the reasons for these changes, it still creates a sense of isolation and disconnectedness for them.

Given all the social drawbacks of being childless, they still feel strongly that it is the right decision for them, and this reassures them that they are being true to their priorities. Megan and Matthew feel a pressure to have a different kind of purpose, to be good at something else. Both admit to being introverted, requiring lots of downtime, and being very stress adverse. Caring for animals fits their personalities and lifestyle, and they decided to start training service dogs. This puts them in a social community of other dog trainers, gives them an opportunity to nurture, and creates challenge and stimulation as they learn the training program. Megan struggles with her non-mother identity and finds that although being a dog trainer and being involved in other interests help fill that void, she realizes that on some level it may be a lifelong struggle.

Going forward, they believe that finding life balance will require vigilance and adaptability. Some of the key features include increasing their social connectedness, lots of travel, meaningful paid or volunteer work, and stimulating hobbies. They recently found a social group called "No Kidding" consisting of other childfree couples to which they have committed. Matthew is active in a community theatre, and they just got a four-month-old puppy to train as a service dog.

Values Clarification Exercise

Try this values clarification exercise to see if your lifestyle is aligned with your values and who you want to be.

Achievement	Knowledge	Religious faith	Others
Altruism	Love	Skill	
Autonomy	Loyalty	Wealth	
Creativity	Environment	Wisdom	
Emotional well being	Physical appearance	Friendship	
Health	Pleasure	Financial security	
Honesty	Power	Competition	
Justice	Recognition	Physical activity	

1. Make a list of ten of your most strongly held personal values from the above list. This list is not comprehensive, so feel free to add additional values you feel are appropriate.

    1. _____ 6. _____
    2. _____ 7. _____
    3. _____ 8. _____
    4. _____ 9. _____
    5. _____ 10. _____

2. Reduce the list to five values. This won't be easy, but really make them count.

    1. _____
    2. _____
    3. _____
    4. _____
    5. _____

3. Now imagine that you can only have three. This is even harder. Which two would you give up? Which would you keep? Why?

    1. _____

    2. _____

    3. _____

4. Take a look at the remaining values on your list. Consider the following questions:

    - What do those values say about you as a person?
    - Do you feel that your lifestyle reflects the values you have identified? Why or why not?
    - Do you see any gaps between your everyday activities and your values?

CHAPTER 9

Things Get in the Way

Martha had intended to go to school for nursing, but when she became pregnant at nineteen years old, her plans were derailed. Her boyfriend bolted, and her parents were divorced. Her mother was struggling with drug addiction, and her father was rarely around. Without the support from her parents, she had to go on public assistance while she took care of her daughter, Tracie. When Tracie was old enough to be in school all day, Martha became certified as a nursing assistant and managed to work the night shift. Her daughter slept at the neighbors, requiring only a minimal payment for care. The nursing assistant job did not pay the bills so she took a second job at a bakery for twenty hours each week while Tracie was in school. Nothing was easy.

Her mother gave her an old car, but it constantly needed repairs, and between that and the expense of gas, she quit using it. There was a bus service two blocks from her house that took her to her nursing assistant job without having to transfer, but she used it during late hours and didn't always feel safe. Once on her way to work, someone stole her wallet out of her backpack, and she didn't realize it until later. The bakery job was at the edge of town and required a transfer to another bus, which added twenty minutes each way to her commute.

Martha is fifty pounds overweight, and when the nurses at work took her blood pressures, they said it was consistently high. The only grocery store near her neighborhood is a mile away and not on her bus route. There is a convenience store and a Burger King on the corner where she catches the bus, so when she comes home, she eats the throwaways from the bakery and convenience foods. Martha knows she needs to eat better and exercise more, but she can hardly muster up the energy to make any changes. Unfortunately, her fifteen-year-old daughter Tracie is also showing signs of unhealthy weight gain.

Sometimes things get in the way, and we don't always have choices in our activities. In Martha's case, most of her cars are in the ditch. Her health is at risk, she is not challenged in her work, and she is not satisfied with her identity. The one area of balance is her positive relationship with her daughter and her coworkers. She is deeply committed to these relationships and feels good about herself when she is with them.

To improve life balance, one of the choices might be to join a fitness center and make a commitment to exercise regularly. This isn't an option for Martha. She doesn't have the time, money, or access. There isn't one near her or on her bus route. To add challenge in life, you might choose to take up a new hobby and learn photography or sculpture or go back to school for a career change. This isn't an easy option for Martha either. Even something as basic as nutritional eating presents barriers to Martha because of the limited resources in her neighborhood. It would be understandable if the idea of life balance does not resonate with Martha because she is too busy trying to survive and life balance is too much of a luxury to consider.

Martha's environment puts up all kinds of barriers to living the healthy and satisfactory life she wants. Her social environment includes her family, friends, coworkers, or anyone she encounters regularly. This network of people represents some of her social capital and can have a large influence on her health and well-being. The rest of her social capital can be found in relationships within her neighborhoods, churches, schools, clubs, civic associations, and even local bars/restaurants. When social capital is expansive and supportive, research shows that people benefit by having better health and well-being.[55]

Kathleen Matuska

People in communities that are highly connected are also more likely to have higher educational achievement and better employment outcomes, and their neighborhoods have lower crime rates.[56] Think about your own life and how your social capital helped you. A few random examples could look like this:

- You found a reliable handyman from the church bulletin.
- Your neighbor told you about a job opening for which you are qualified.
- Your cousin shared a wonderful, low-cost, easy recipe on social media.
- The local police know you and wave as they pass you on the walk.
- Your child's teacher calls you with updates on progress.
- You discovered a convenient, low-cost emergency childcare setting at a nearby community center.
- Your friend brings you a meal when she finds out you are ill.

These are only a few simple examples, but you can see how even these minor connections can add up to a feeling of support and well-being. Of course social capital can also make a difference in larger areas of your life, like your career or housing. Social networking is viewed as one of the best ways to land the job you want, and you'll see lots of websites describing how to increase your social network for that purpose.

On the other hand, when social capital is limited and relationships are stressful or unsupportive, people are more likely to have mental or physical health problems.[57,58] Martha enjoys her daughter and coworkers, but she rarely talks to her neighbors except the one who lets Tracie sleep there at night. She doesn't belong to any community groups, and her parents and extended family are not supportive. She would like to attend church services but often has to work on Sundays, and if she is not working, she really prefers to catch up on her sleep. In her case, she can count on very few people for support, and she misses out on the useful advice and resources from people in the community. All of this is a vicious circle where Martha could become increasingly isolated and marginalized, which diminishes her well-being and so on.

Your physical and economic environments can also influence life balance. Swedish researchers found that, when people were describing their ideas of a balanced life, most included financial security as important.[22] The Swedish participants in the study reported that not having enough money was one of the biggest barriers to doing what they wanted to do. Of course, when you don't have enough money, it also limits your choices for how and where you live. The World Health Organization (WHO) recognizes that people live, grow, work, and age in different conditions, and when there are poor conditions, there are unfair and avoidable differences in health and well-being.[59]

In addition to the social isolation, the physical characteristics of Martha's neighborhood constrain her choices for healthy activities. Researchers have found that the availability of fresh food markets, recreational resources like parks and walking or biking paths, and a sense of security when in the neighborhood relates to lower stress, better health, and more life satisfaction.[60] When people live in neighborhoods where they are constantly afraid of being robbed or attacked, their stress levels are always running high, and of course this contributes to poor health.[61]

People don't typically choose these stressful conditions but are forced to live in unhealthy neighborhoods because of low income, putting them at a disadvantage for all the negative health consequences. It's not that it is impossible to increase exercise or eat healthier when someone is poor. It just requires more resources, effort, and planning and may be just too big of a barrier when life gets hard.

These poorer neighborhoods are disproportionality home to people of color. The Risk Factor Survey of approximately thirty communities in the United States indicated that residents in mostly minority communities continue to have lower socioeconomic status, greater barriers to health-care access, and greater risks for and burden of disease compared with the general population living in the same county or state.[59] For example, if you are black, you are 50 percent more likely to die of heart disease or stroke prematurely (before the age of seventy-five years) than if you are non-Hispanic white. Similarly, if you are black or Hispanic, you are more likely to have diabetes than other groups. Diabetes is also more common for people who have lower household incomes and/or a less than a high school education. Even infant death rates are different across racial groups, with blacks having significantly higher rates than non-Hispanic whites. Rates of infant deaths also vary geographically with higher rates in the South and Midwest than in other parts of the country.[59] This disparity among groups cannot be explained by anything other than the differences in resources or opportunities available to them.

Another aspect of your environment is culture. We don't always recognize our own cultural values and expectations because they are so ingrained in everyday living. By its very nature, culture shapes our lives and plays out in activities in ways that may be invisible to us most of the time. Culture is generally noticed when it is different from your own. An unfamiliar person or group has a different culture, but you may not recognize your own culture that is seen as different to others.

One of the problems about the concept of life balance is that it has been created and studied primarily by scientists in Western cultures. I was so excited about the topic that, at first, I was certain that this would be important to everyone. After all we are all human and have the same needs and desires, right? It took me a while to recognize that the values and attitudes surrounding the concept of life balance may not resonate with everyone. In fact it may seem narcissistic to some. The idea of an individual's concern about satisfaction with time spent in desired activities may seem totally inappropriate and incomprehensible to people from certain cultures.

A good example might be people who have collectivist values, as in several non-Western communities. In collectivist cultures, there is a priority of group goals over individual goals, so one's sense of life balance may not really matter. Life balance, as this book describes, takes a very individual approach, and people look inward to examine satisfaction with their lives. In collectivist cultures, individuals don't think about their personal satisfaction, except for how they have contributed to the well-being of the group. Future research should examine whether there is a community or family balance construct that resonates with people in collectivist cultures and how it should be defined and measured.

If the idea of having a balanced life resonates with you and appeals to you, you have choices to make every day. I am arguing that it is not a static state that you achieve and keep, but an aspiration and guide to living that helps you make life choices to improve your overall well-being. You can make small or large changes that start with developing the skill to do so. Even with environmental constraints, there may still be some things you can control to improve your life balance, but it has to come from you.

I return to the metaphor of your road of life with cars representing how your daily activities are meeting your needs. Imagine poor driving conditions, like snow, that force you to drive more cautiously and may even make one car slide into the ditch. There are things you can control and things you cannot. You can put snow tires on the car, change the time you drive, drive slower, or avoid it all together, but you cannot make it stop snowing.

NawLer

Life balance is "when I am able to take care of everything at home, work and school" NawLer lived in a refugee camp in Thailand until she was twenty-four years old. She was born in Burma and at six months old, her parents fled with her and her ten siblings to Thailand seeking safety and hoping for a better life. The refugee camp was the only home she knew, staying twenty-four years before immigrating to the United States. NawLer believes the camp was good in many ways because her family could be together. There was a strong sense of community among the residents, housing and food was provided, and children could go to school. Educational opportunities were inaccessible for her parents and grandparents who lived in remote villages in Burma so they are very supportive of their children going to school as a road to a better life.

Even though basic needs were met, NawLer felt people were stifled and stuck in the camps with no real employment or challenge. No one was allowed to leave. She knew of some individuals who tried to leave the camp to look for jobs and were caught by police, imprisoned, and never seen again.

When she arrived in the United States nine years ago, she settled with her family in a Minnesota community close to other new immigrants. The barriers and obstacles to everyday living were everywhere in NawLer's world, but she described herself as very hard-working and persistent, personality traits that helped her navigate an unfamiliar world. She also had the support and encouragement from her large family and community. She enrolled in classes to learn the English language because she felt isolated from the larger community. Although her English is still broken, she has enough command of the language that she serves as an interpreter for her family and community.

She then enrolled in classes to become an American citizen and jokes about how hard the exam questions were. NawLer relied on her older brothers to teach her to drive. With no previous expose to traffic, high speeds and interstate roads, it took a lot of courage and determination to take and pass the driver's exam.

Even something as basic as writing checks and paying bills was new for NawLer and she had to learn about banking, saving, and budgeting. NawLer shared that one of her most stressful periods was when she forgot to pay a bill and ended up incurring a late fee. That experience was painful for her, and she was frustrated with all the new things she had to learn. She wants to have a good job so she is taking classes at a local community college with hopes of earning an associate's degree in child development.

NawLer has worked hard to find the sweet spot between two cultures. She agrees that her collectivist Karen culture sometimes clashes with the individualistic Western culture. She is married and has noticed that Karen culture seems to have more equality between the husband and the wife. The husband is traditionally the breadwinner, and the wife manages all the money and the children. Decisions are made jointly, and they both do the housework. She appreciates that there is a lot of mutual respect between them.

NawLer's widowed mother lives with her. In the Karen tradition, elder family members live with their adult children or relatives, but typically it is with the youngest. Having her Mother live with them is a big help because she does most of the cooking. This is a relief when NawLer is multitasking with school, work, and parenting. On weekends the house is usually filled with family who are visiting her mother, a traditional value that NawLer will not interfere with. Her family and community are her highest priorities and her own desires are put on hold when the family gathers. She says it can be stressful

when she has an upcoming exam and needs time to study, but she waits until they leave, studying late in the night. This is why NawLer said the key to a balanced life is to have good time management. She has learned to squeeze time for her own goals in-between the time demands of her family and community.

NawLer relates to the concept of life balance and appreciates when she can manage everything without stress. She has aspirations to continue her education toward a career and expresses gratitude for being in the United States where these freedoms are possible. She values her roles of wife and mother with big dreams for her children's future. It was also very evident to me that NawLer's community supports her as much as she encourages them. In order to feel balanced, NawLer wants to meet all her needs but her own well-being is also dependent on the health and well-being of her family.

My Environment

Social/Cultural Environment

Have you ever thought about your social capital? As you can see in this chapter, it is actually worth knowing because your social capital is related to health and well-being. With whom do you have a common bond? This would be people who share a common identity with you. List people from your neighborhood, your work or volunteer group, your family and friends, and virtual/online networks.

With whom do you share other interests or activities? This would be people who may be very different from you or people you don't know as well as the group above. You recognize them and could easily have a conversation about something you have in common. List people from your neighborhood/community, your work or volunteer group, your church, extended family/acquaintances, and virtual/online networks.

With whom do you interact regarding political, economic, or other important facets of your life? This could be groups further up or lower down the social ladder. List people from your community, your work or volunteer group, your church, and civic organizations.

Examine your list. Do you have people or groups listed in all of the categories? Where are your strongest supports? Where are your weakest supports?

Physical/Economic Environment

How does your physical environment influence your daily activities? Think about each of the following in your neighborhood:

- Do you have places to walk or bike safely (uncluttered sidewalks and trails)?
- Are there attractive green spaces available to enjoy (parks and walkways)?

- Are groceries stores nearby?
- Is transportation convenient?
- Are there enrichment opportunities such as libraries, community centers, or schools?
- Do you feel safe?
- Is there clean air and water?
- Is it quiet when you need rest?

CHAPTER 10

Making It Work

In this book you have learned that there are many ways that scientists view life balance. There are also a few commonalities that at least five researchers can agree with. Life balance is a journey, not a destination. It is different for everyone. It requires doing things. It is good for you. And sometimes life makes it difficult. In each of these agreements, the recurring theme is the importance of everyday activities. What you do from day to day has the potential to influence your overall health and well-being. You know you need to include fruits and vegetables in your daily diet for nutritional health, but are you attentive to doing things that meet your needs on a regular basis for your overall health? Sprinkling your life with regular activities that support your need for physical health, positive relationships, challenge, and a positive identity will go a long way toward balancing your life and reducing your stress. But because life can be unpredictable and just plain difficult at times, you are not always successful in meeting those needs.

In the LBM discussed in chapter 4, meeting your four needs is only one of the components of a balanced life. The other equally important component is the ability to match what you do and what you want to do as much as possible. This part requires a certain skill that I believe can be learned. It doesn't take away the fact that there are real barriers to matching what you do and what you want to do. The intent is to do as much as possible to move in a more balanced state, knowing it will never be perfect. Even in extremely stressful or constrained environments, it may still be possible to do something that helps you feel more balanced or at least buffer some of your stress.

Awareness

The skill in moving toward a balanced life involves awareness, attention, and motivation. After reading this book, you are aware that meeting your four needs through your daily activities is important for your overall health and well-being. That's the first step. Behavior change occurs when you are aware that you need to change and believe that change will result in a better outcome. Do you believe that you can find a more satisfying pattern of activities in your life? If so, do you think it will result in less stress or improved well-being?

Attention

The second step requires that you pay attention to what you are doing from day to day and be alert to the resources around you. Is there a match between what you want to do and what you are actually doing? This step can be harder because being attentive means you need to take time to reflect and process, a habit that is not nurtured in modern society. When you think about your cars going down the road, are they all in the middle? That metaphor is a good one for people who just let the busyness of life take over and are not in control of slowing down or redirecting their cars. Being attentive means to pause and think about what you are doing and comparing that to your needs. Here are some questions you can ask yourself during your reflection:

- What am I doing to meet my health needs?
- How do I feel about the important relationships in my life?

- Am I bored or unstimulated?
- Do I feel good about the identity I've created?

Take the LBI from chapter 4 and reflect on your results. Of course knowing where you may need to change doesn't always lead to actual change. There are lots of legitimate reasons for this, one being that change requires too much effort when energy levels are low or tensions are high. Your environment provides lots of barriers, and it takes alertness to notice things that can help you overcome the barriers. For example, if you have been feeling dissatisfied with your relationship with your father because you rarely call him, you may make a pledge to call him more regularly. That might work for a while, but if it were sustainable, why didn't it work in the past? You will have better luck if you use the resources in your environment to help you. Social media and email, which you use regularly, are easy ways to stay in touch without changing your habits. Perhaps teaching your father to use these resources will keep you connected in new ways. Making a commitment to do something new, like playing the clarinet two or three times a week, doesn't necessarily happen just because you will it. But if you build in supports for your new habit, like finding a community band to join, the motivation to maintain the habit increases. Creating new exercise habits are often more successful if done with someone else. You are more likely to wake up early to take a walk if you know someone is waiting for you. Being alert to and taking advantage of these opportunities that will help you is a skill you can develop.

Motivation and Goal Setting

The third step requires motivation to change (the difficult part) and occurs through effective goal setting. The first goal-setting principle is to make goals easy enough to achieve so motivation follows. They should be realistic and achievable. For example, if you have had very little exercise in the past few years but decide you want to increase your fitness level, then declaring "I will run every day for thirty minutes" will set you up for failure if you are not already in the habit. If you missed only one day, you will feel like you did not meet your goal, it is impossible to do, and you will likely quit all together.

On the other hand, if you are very careful about setting a realistic goal, you will have more success. "I will follow a beginner runner training schedule (walk/run sequence) at least once on the weekend and once after work for the next six months." This goal allows life to happen in between running and is probably achievable, thus increasing your motivation to continue. Achieving small goals builds confidence and makes it more likely the activities will become part of your habits and lifestyle. Goals can continue to push you, and once you've achieved the smaller goal, you can build on it to become the runner you want to be. "I will run two miles three times per week for the next six months."

The second goal-setting principle is to make the goals very clear and measureable so you know exactly what behavior is expected. A goal like "I will be more physically fit" will not be helpful for you because it is too broad. You will be much more successful if you pick a behavior that you think you would enjoy and disrupts your life as little as possible. Instead of suddenly becoming physically fit, start with a very measureable goal, like "I will stand while working on the computer for at least one hour each day" or "I will walk for twenty minutes over my lunch hour, three days a week" With these types of goals, you know what you are supposed to do, and you know if you've met the goal or not. They are also built into your current activities and therefore more likely to be followed.

I am a goal setter, so much so that I even have a list of small goals in my head every day when I wake up. At the end of the day, I can feel good about the goals I have achieved. I have large goals ("I will write a book within the year"), and I have small goals ("I will call my adult children today and make plans for Thanksgiving"). I used to think that everyone was naturally a goal setter, but I have discovered that is not necessarily true. I believe, in order to have a life journey with more periods of balance than not, people need to pay attention to their activity choices and set goals to make small changes to increase satisfaction and meet their needs.

Goal Setting Exercise

This exercise will help you develop the skills needed to match what you are doing to what you want to be doing. Take baby steps toward a more balanced life.

Increase Your Knowledge

Take the LBI and print out your results. (You will lose them once you log off.) You will find it at this address: http://minerva.stkate.edu/lbi.nsf.

Pay Attention

Examine the results. What need areas (health, relationships, challenge, and identity) have the lowest scores? Choose one activity area in which you are not satisfied, where you spend too little or too much time doing. List the resources in your environment that might help you become more satisfied with the time you spend in that activity.

Find the Motivation

Write a measureable and realistic goal that you can obtain in three months. Break that goal down even farther, and write a stepping-stone goal that will get you to your three-month goal. Do it!

BIBLIOGRAPHY

1. Mathiowetz, V., K. M. Matuska, and M. E. Murphy. "Efficacy of an Energy Conservation Course for Persons with Multiple Sclerosis." *Arch Phys Med Rehabil* 82(4)(2001): 449–456, doi: 10.1053/apmr.2001.22192.

2. Mathiowetz, V. G., M. L. Finlayson, K. M. Matuska, Y. C. Hua, and P. Luo. "Randomized Controlled Trial of an Energy Conservation Course for Persons with Multiple Sclerosis." *Multiple Sclerosis* 11(5)(2005): 592–601, doi: 10.1191/1352458505ms1198oa.

3. Matuska, K., V. Mathiowetz, and M. Finlayson. "Use and Perceived Effectiveness of Energy Conservation Strategies for Managing Multiple Sclerosis Fatigue." *The American Journal of Occupational Therapy* 61(1)(2007): 62–69.

4. Christiansen, C. H., and K. M. Matuska. "Lifestyle Balance: A Review of Concepts and Research." *Journal of Occupational Science* 13(1)(2006): 49–61, doi: 10.1080/14427591.2006.9686570.

5. Matuska, K., and C. Christiansen. "A Proposed Model of Lifestyle Balance." *Journal of Occupational Science* 15(1)(2008): 9–19.

6. Selye, H. *The Stress of Life*, rev. ed. New York: McGraw-Hill, 1976.

7. McEwen, B. S., and J. C. Wingfield. "The Concept of Allostasis in Biology and Biomedicine." *Horm Behav* 43(1)(2003): 2–15, doi: 10.1016/S0018-506X(02)00024-7.

8. Wheeler, R. J., and M. A. Frank. "Identification of Stress Buffers." *Behav Med* 14(2)(1988): 78–89.

9. Gerber, M., M. Kellmann, T. Hartmann, and U. Pühs. "Do Exercise and Fitness Buffer Against Stress Among Swiss Police and

Emergency Response Service Officers?" *Psychol Sport Exerc* 11(4) (2010): 286–294.

10. Hamilton N. A., D. Catley, and C. Karlson. "Sleep and the Affective Response to Stress and Pain." *Health Psychology* 26(3)(2007): 288–295, doi: 10.1037/0278-6133.26.3.288.

11. Rueggeberg, R., C. Wrosch, and G. E. Miller. "Sleep Duration Buffers Diurnal Cortisol Increases in Older Adulthood." *Psychoneuroendocrinology* 37(7)(2012): 1029–1038, doi: 10.1016/j.psyneuen.2011.11.012 [doi].

12. Iso-Ahola, S., and C. J. Park. "Leisure-Related Social Support and Self-Determination as Buffers of Stress-Illness Relationship." *J Leisure Res* 28(1996): 169.

13. Schwarzer, R., R. M. Bowler, and J. E. Cone. "Social Integration Buffers Stress in New York Police After the 9/11 Terrorist Attack." *Anxiety Stress Coping* 27(1)(2014): 18–26, doi: 10.1080/10615806.2013.806652.

14. Linville, P. W. "Self-Complexity as a Cognitive Buffer Against Stress-Related Illness and Depression." *J Pers Soc Psychol* 52(4) (1987): 663–676, doi: 10.1037/0022-3514.52.4.663.

15. Goode, W. J. "A Theory of Role Strain." *Am Sociol Rev* 25(4)(1960): 483–496.

16. Marks, S. R., and S. M. MacDermid. "Multiple Roles and the Self: A Theory of Role Balance." *Journal of Marriage and the Family* 58(2)(1996): 417.

17. Persson, D., and H. Jonsson. "The Importance of Experienced Challenges in a Balanced Life—Micro and Macro Perspectives." In *Life Balance: Multidisciplinary Theories and Research*, edited by K. Matuska and C. Christiansen, 147–161. Bethesda; Thorofare, NJ: AOTA Press; Slack, Inc., 2009.

18. Csikszentmihalyi, M. *Living Well. The Psychology of Everyday Life.* London: Phoenix Books, 1997.

19. *Flow: The Psychology of Optimal Experience*, 1st ed. New York: Harper and Row, 1990.

20. Wagman, P., C. Håkansson, C. Jacobsson, T. Falkmer, and A. Björklund. "What Is Considered Important for Life Balance? Similarities and Differences among Some Working Adults." *Scand J Occup Ther* 19(4)(2012): 377–384, doi: 10.3109/11038128.2011.645552.

21. Håkansson. C, and K. M. Matuska. "How Life Balance Is Perceived by Swedish Women Recovering from a Stress-Related Disorder: A Validation of the Life Balance Model." *Journal of Occupational Science* 17(2)(2010): 112–119, doi: 10.1080/14427591.2010.9686682.

22. Wagman, P., C. Håkansson, K. M. Matuska, A. Björklund, and T. Falkmer. "Validating the Model of Lifestyle Balance on a Working Swedish Population." *Journal of Occupational Science* 19(2)(2012): 106–114, doi: 10.1080/14427591.2011.575760.

23. Wagman, P., C. Håkansson, and A. Björklund. "Occupational Balance as Used in Occupational Therapy: A Concept Analysis." *Scand J Occup Ther* 19(4)(2012): 322–327, doi: 10.3109/11038128.2011.596219.

24. Wada, M., C. L. Backman, S. J. Forwell, W. Roth, and J. J. Ponzetti. "Balance in Everyday Life: Dual-Income Parents' Collective and Individual Conceptions." *Journal of Occupational Science* 21(3) (2014): 259–276, doi: 10.1080/14427591.2014.913331.

25. Stamm, T., L. Lovelock, G. Stew, et al. "I Have a Disease But I Am Not Ill: A Narrative Study of Occupational Balance in People with Rheumatoid Arthritis." *OTJR: Occupation, Participation and Health* 29(1)(2009): 32–39.

26. Anaby, D. R., Backman, C. L., and T. Jarus. "Measuring Occupational Balance: A Theoretical Exploration of Two Approaches." *The Canadian Journal of Occupational Therapy* 77(5)(2010): 280–288.

27. Pentland, W., and M. McColl. "Another Perspective on Life Balance— Living in Integrity with Values." In *Life Balance: Multidisciplinary Theories and Research*, edited by K. Matuska and C. Christiansen, 165–180. Bethesda; Thorofare, NJ: AOTA Press; Slack, Inc., 2009.

28. Veenhoven, R. "Optimal Lifestyle-Mix: An Inductive Approach." In *Life Balance: Multidisciplinary Theories and Research*, edited by

K. Matuska and C. Christiansen. Bethesda; Thorofare, NJ.: AOTA Press; Slack, Inc., 2009.

29. Sheldon, K. M., and C. P. Niemiec. "It's Not Just the Amount That Counts: Balanced Need Satisfaction Also Affects Well-Being." *J Pers Soc Psychol* 91(2)(2006): 331–341, doi: 10.1037/0022-3514.91.2.331.

30. Sheldon, K. M., R. Cummins, and S. Kamble. "Life Balance and Well-Being: Testing a Novel Conceptual and Measurement Approach." *J Pers* 78(4)(2010): 1093–1134, doi: 10.1111/j.1467-6494.2010.00644.x.

31. Matuska, K. "Validity Evidence of a Model and Measure of Life Balance." *OTJR: Occupation, Participation and Health* 32(1)(2012): 229–237, doi: 10.3928/15394492-0110610-02.

32. Matuska, K., J. Bass, and J. V. Schmitt. "Life Balance and Perceived Stress: Predictors and Demographic Profile." *OTJR: Occupation, Participation and Health* 33(3)(2013): 146–158, doi: 10.3928/15394492-20130614-03.

33. Matuska, K. "Description and Development of the Life Balance Inventory." *OTJR: Occupation, Participation and Health* 32(1) (2012): 220–228, doi: 10.3928/15394492-20110610-01.

34. Bureau of Labor Statistics. "American Time Use Survey—2014 Results." USDL-15-1236, 2015.

35. National Alliance for Caregiving and AARP. "Caregiving in the U.S. 2009." 2009.

36. Hoffman, E., S. Kaneshiro, and W. C. Compton. "Peak-Experiences Among Americans in Midlife." *Journal of Humanistic Psychology* 52(4)(2012): 479–503, doi: 10.1177/0022167811433851.

37. Strauch, B. *The Secret Life of the Grown-up Brain: Surprising Talents of the Middle-Aged Mind.* New York: Penguin, 2011.

38. Jonsson, H. "The Retirement Process in an Occupational Perspective: A Review of Literature and Theories." *Physical & Occupational Therapy in Geriatrics* (1993).

39. Guinn, B. "Leisure Behavior Motivation and the Life Satisfaction of Retired Persons." *Activities, Adaptations, and Aging* 23(1999): 13–20.

40. Jonsson, H., L. Borell, and G. Sadlo. "Retirement: An Occupational Transition with Consequences for Temporality, Balance and Meaning of Occupations." *Journal of Occupational Science* 7(1) (2000): 29–37, doi: 10.1080/14427591.2000.9686462.

41. Clark, F., D. Parham, M. Carlson, et al. "Occupational Science: Academic Innovation in the Service of Occupational Therapy's Future." *American Journal of Occupational Therapy* 45(4)(1991): 300–310.

42. National Institute of Health. "Overweight and Obesity Statistics." Accessed October 29, 2015. http://www.niddk.nih.gov/health-information/health-statistics/Pages/overweight-obesity-statistics.aspx.

43. Matuska, K., J. Bass. "Life Balance and Stress in Adults with Medical Conditions or Obesity." *Occupational Therapy Journal of Research: Occupation, Participation, and Health* (2016).

44. World Health Organization. "International Classification of Functioning, Disability, and Health (ICF)." Accessed October 29, 2015. http://www.who.int/classifications/icf/en/.

45. Clark, F., S. Azen, R. Zemke, et al. "Occupational Therapy for Independent-Living Older Adults: A Randomized Controlled Trial." *Journal of the American Medical Association* 278 (1997): 1321–1326.

46. Clark, F., J. Jackson, M. Carlson, et al. "Effectiveness of a Lifestyle Intervention in Promoting the Well-Being of Independently Living Older People: Results of the Well Elderly 2 Randomised Controlled trial." *Journal of Epidemiology and Community Health* 66(9)(2012): 782–790.

47. Matuska, K., A. Giles-Heinz, N. Flinn, M. Neighbor, and J. Bass-Haugen. "Outcomes of a Pilot Occupational Therapy Wellness Program for Older Adults." *Am J Occup Ther* 57(2)(2003): 220–224.

48. Gupta, J., and C. Sullivan. "The Central Role of Occupation in the Doing, Being and Belonging of Immigrant women." *Journal of Occupational Science* 20(1)(2013): 23–35, doi: 10.1080/14427591.2012.717499.

49. Digman, J. M. "Personality Structure: Emergence of the Five-Factor Model." *Annu Rev Psychol* 41(1)(1990): 417.

50. Costa P. T, Jr., and R. R. McCrae. "From Catalog to Classification: Murray's Needs and the Five-Factor Model." *J Pers Soc Psychol* 55(2) (1988): 258–265, doi: 10.1037/0022-3514.55.2.258.

51. Kraaykamp, G., and K. V. Eijck. "Personality, Media Preferences, and Cultural Participation." *Personality and Individual Differences* 38(7)(2005): 1675–1688, doi: 10.1016/j.paid.2004.11.002.

52. Mehmetoglu, M. "Personality Effects on Experiential Consumption." *Personality and Individual Differences* 52(1): 94–99.

53. Zeigler-Hill, V., and S. Monica. "The HEXACO Model of Personality and Video Game Preferences." *Entertainment Computing* 11: 21–26.

54. Rentfrow, P. J., and S. D. Gosling. "The Do Re Mi's of Everyday Life: The Structure and Personality Correlates of Music Preferences." *J Pers Soc Psychol* 84(6)(2003): 1236–1256, doi: 10.1037/0022-3514.84.6.1236.

55. McNeill, L. H., Kreuter M. W., and S. V. Subramanian. "Social Environment and Physical Activity: A Review of Concepts and Evidence." *Soc Sci Med* 63(4)(2006): 1011–1022.

56. Eisenberger, N. I., and S. W. Cole. "Social Neuroscience and Health: Neurophysiological Mechanisms Linking Social Ties with Physical Health." *Nat Neurosci* 15(5)(2012): 669–674, doi: 10.1038/nn.3086.

57. Holt-Lunstad, J., T. B. Smith, M. Baker, T. Harris, and D. Stephenson. "Loneliness and Social Isolation as Risk Factors for Mortality: A Meta-Analytic Review." *Perspectives on Psychological Science* 10(2)(2015): 227–237, doi: 10.1177/1745691614568352.

58. Holt-Lunstad, J., T. B. Smith, and J. B. Layton. "Social Relationships and Mortality Risk: A Meta-Analytic Review." *PLoS medicine* 7(7) (2010): e1000316, doi: 10.1371/journal.pmed.1000316.

59. Centers for Disease Control and Prevention. "CDC Health Disparities and Inequalities Report—United States, 2013." MMWR 2013; 62(Suppl 3).

60. Dulin, M. F., and H. Tapp. "Communities Matter: The Relationship between Neighborhoods and Health." *N C Med J* 73(5)(2012): 381.

61. Ross, C. E., and J. Mirowsky. "Neighborhood Disadvantage, Disorder, and Health." *J Health Soc Behav* 42(3)(2001): 258–276.

CPSIA information can be obtained
at www.ICGtesting.com
Printed in the USA
FFOW04n0705280117
31798FF